T0106244

CALLSIGN: SPECTRE

CALLSIGN: SPECTRE

JEFF NOECKER

iUniverse, Inc.
Bloomington

Callsign: Spectre

iUniverse books may be ordered through booksellers or by contacting:

iUniverse
1663 Liberty Drive
Bloomington, IN 47403
www.iuniverse.com
1-800-Authors (1-800-288-4677)

ISBN: 978-1-4620-0482-9 (sc)
ISBN: 978-1-4620-0483-6 (dj)
ISBN: 978-1-4620-0484-3 (ebk)

Library of Congress Control Number: 2011904125

Printed in the United States of America

iUniverse rev. date: 04/17/2012

DEDICATION

This story is dedicated to all Spectres, past and present, whether aircrew, maintainers, or administrators. These were true warriors who took a humble cargo airplane and turned it into one of the deadliest attack aircraft ever known.

But a special dedication goes out to Dale Compton and his wife, Ellen, without whose enthusiastic encouragement this book may never have been written. Dale was on my crew, and in his case, the use of the phrase, "comrade-in-arms," would be an understatement. Throughout my entire air force career, I've never met anyone with Dale's dedication to the job or to his fellow workers. And in a combat environment, this trait proves to be invaluable. If during a mission a fellow gunner made any type of comment to the effect that he was having trouble with a gun or anything else at his position, Dale was there in a second, whether he was asked to or not. If a performance report had a section labeled reliability, Dale would have received the highest score.

After thirty-eight years, Dale found me via the Spectre Association Website and e-mailed me blind. Since that September of 2009, our friendship has bloomed and turned into a remarkable relationship. As with most combat veterans, Dale and I had our demons after leaving Southeast Asia. We had our share of dreams and nightmares that often left us screaming unintelligible things in our sleep, much to the chagrin of any relative within earshot. One cannot truly exorcize these demons by oneself or with the help of anyone not closely associated with the unit and its mission. It is part of the price you must pay if what you do is classified and you are sworn to secrecy. Even without the secrecy, trying to explain our experiences to "gunship laymen" can lead to very unkind observations by those persons. Both of us have experienced being called braggarts and/or being accused of making up and embellishing stories. These accusations became very painful, and we learned to shut up and allowed all these "attacks" to stew for decades rather than be humiliated or accused of tap dancing while we tried to explain. Having found each other again has been a psychological panacea for both of us. We both concede that the other has a great ear and huge shoulders on which to lean. It's fair to say that most, if not all, of the demons have finally been exorcised.

Here's a bit of trivia on my airborne foxhole mate:

Entered the air force in 1969 and separated in 1973. He was promoted to staff sergeant with fewer than four years' service.
Officially, Dale flew ninety-eight combat missions. But, as in my case, he's relatively certain that the actual figure is higher.

Decorations/Medals:
    5 Distinguished Flying Crosses
    4 Air Medals
    Basic Aircrew Wings awarded December 24, 1970

Career Highlights:
    Weapons Mechanic Tech School (TAC), Lowry AFB—December 1969
    Airborne Weapons Technician (AC-130A), Lockbourne AFB—June 1970
    Survival Training S-V80-A, Fairchild AFB—July 1970
    PACAF Jungle Survival School, Clark AFB—September 1970

After his tour in gunships, Dale rotated back to the States and was fortunate enough to be stationed in places that allowed him to keep in close contact with the gunship program and community. Here's a sampling:

Operation and Maintenance Howitzer, M102, 105 mm. Department of the Army Weapons Command, Rock Island, Illinois. July 1972

AC130 105MM Prototype Trainable Gun Mount, Delco Electronics, Division of General Motors, Milwaukee, Wisconsin. August 1972

Dale received an Honorable Discharge on April 1973. A direct quote from Dale exclaimed the following, "Nixon offered me a three-month early out, I took it and hauled ass for Dallas." (Dale always had a difficult time expressing himself.)

With the early out, Dale's total active service was three years, nine months, and fourteen days.

There seems to be a lot of references to foxholes in my story. The reason behind that is something I don't mind explaining. There's a sports network up here in the Northeast called YES: Yankee's Entertainment and Sports Network. In addition to broadcasting the majority of New York's professional sports teams' games, they offer a plethora of shows dealing with the teams specifically and local sports in general. Another one of their offerings is a talk show. The guests are always celebrities, but not always in sports. The host asks the questions, and the guests often reveal facts that were unknown to the public until their appearance on the show. At the very end of the show, the host has a segment called "Hit and Run." The host asks a pertinent question, and the celebrity must answer quickly with the first thing that comes into his head. The questions range from favorite movie to what snack they eat in front of the TV at midnight. But the one question that never changes is the last question: "If you were in a foxhole and in a desperate situation, who would you want with you to help you get out of the situation?" I've had very good, close friends since my time in gunships and been very close to a lot of these people. I love these people dearly and know I can always rely on their friendship. However, I've never been in combat with them. At the risk of insulting or alienating some of these folks, if asked the foxhole question, my answer would always be Dale Compton. Why? Been there, done that in combat with Dale. I survived aerial combat and lived to tell the tale. Am I saying it's all due to Dale? Of course not. But, his reliability and attention to detail while under pressure in a combat environment didn't go unnoticed. Sam's Hams had the reputation of being one of the smoothest gun crews in the unit.

During the initial writing of the manuscript, Dale Compton was informed he had nasopharyngeal cancer. During the year since the book went live he had beaten it with aggressive chemo and radiation therapy. However, several months later it recurred in several other locations. After several months and six more rounds of chemo, he had beaten it again. The day after he returned home from post-chemo treatment, he succumbed to an after effect at the site of original cancer that no one saw coming nor could have imagined. Dale passed away on 9 April 2012. Rest in peace, brother. You will be missed.

CONTENTS

Introduction 1

Chapter 1—Birth of a Concept. 3

Chapter 2—The Airframes 5

Chapter 3—The Air Force, the Gunship, and Me 12

Chapter 4—The Training and the Crews. 16

Chapter 5—The First Survival School 23

Chapter 6—Jungle Survival School. 36

Chapter 7—Arriving in Southeast Asia 46

Chapter 8—The First Mission. 49

Chapter 9—The Escorts 54

Chapter 10—Colonel Sam 59

Chapter 11—The *First Lady* 105

Chapter 12—Tchepone 113

Chapter 13—The General. 117

Chapter 14—Spectre's Urban Legends 120

Chapter 15—Our Big, Their Bigger 132

Chapter 16—Critters and Party Suits 136

Chapter 17—The Land of Smiles 140

Chapter 18—The Thai Military. 143

Chapter 19—*Prometheus*. 146

Chapter 20—The Rescue Attempt. 149

Chapter 21—Going Home. 151

Epilogue 157

Conclusion 159

Glossary 161

Acknowledgements 166

INTRODUCTION

---⭐---

Nearly forty years after the fact, and with some prodding by friends and family, I have decided to put my combat flight experiences from the Vietnam conflict in print. There have been many military folks who have written about their experiences there, but in this instance, the airplane and the mission sets this story apart from all the others. Within the air force alone at that time, there were hundreds of F-4s, F-105s, B-52s, OV-10, O-2s, A-7s, and any number of other types of aircraft that flew in support of the efforts in Southeast Asia. And there were numerous units to which these aircraft were assigned. But in 1971, there were only fourteen AC-130A gunships in theater and only one squadron to which they belonged. There were even fewer than fourteen when the program began in 1968, and the first few flew out of a base in Vietnam. But, the proximity of "in-country" danger to such expensive resources ultimately saw them transferred out of harm's way to Thailand. At the time, the cost of refitting a C-130 into a gunship version was more expensive than the price of a new B-52. And commensurate with that move, a new unit was formed. The new unit was the 16th Special Ops. Even today, its descendant still operates gunships under the same squadron designation.

This is the story of these magnificent airplanes and the nut cases who flew in them during the Vietnam conflict. The term "nut case" is used with affection, but the crews of this airplane joyfully did things that most rational people would never do. We not only placed our hands on the hot burner of the stove, we sat on it.

The story more closely resembles a diary rather than an autobiography or other form of nonfiction work. It is told in two formats, as if telling the story to a friend over a cup of coffee. The first format is from the author's personal experience. The second is in the form of stories he's heard that sound factual enough and have an entertainment value, although he did not personally witness or confirm them. GIs have the reputation of embellishing their tales, so the author attempts to keep the story as factual as possible. For the reader with a skeptical mind-set, some aspects of the story may seem a bit farfetched and fictional. Even I, who flew on the missions, had a hard time believing some of it while I was actually doing it. Unbelievable as it may sound, the story is unmistakably true.

CHAPTER 1

⭐

BIRTH OF A CONCEPT

The young US Air Force officer, an adviser to a South American country, found himself in the company of a local guide in the Andes. His mission on this particular day was to acclimate himself to the local people and customs. Upon reaching a small plateau at the top of the mountain, he noticed a group of the indigenous people gathered near the center of the plateau, looking skyward. His curiosity piqued, he inquired what was going on. The guide replied that it was mail day. The young officer, with a very quizzical look, responded, "Okay, I'll bite. What is mail day on the top of a mountain?" The guide smiled and said that the people were waiting on the airplane that delivers and picks up mail. Looking at the terrain, the officer quickly noted that there was no room for even the smallest of short takeoff and landing (STOL) aircraft to land or take off from the miniscule plateau. His curiosity growing ever stronger, the young man sat on a nearby rock and waited. For a short time, he wondered if he was being "had." But within a few minutes, he heard the sound of an aircraft engine droning in the distance. Looking up, he saw a rather small, slow aircraft approach and begin circling overhead. The airplane appeared to be a Piper Cub. But, the aircraft was making no attempt to decrease altitude and airspeed to begin a landing approach. It simply began circling the plateau at a steady altitude. Suddenly, something appeared outside

3

the pilot's window and started coming down slowly. As the young officer stood and strained to make out the object, he saw that it was a bucket suspended on a rope. The bucket finally touched the ground, and the locals grabbed it. The pilot then began to fly in a circle around the bucket, making an ever-increasing swath until the bucket was in the center of the turn. With the bucket still attached to the airplane by the rope, the locals began removing the delivered mail and replacing it with their outgoing letters and packages. Having had flight training, the young officer realized he was witnessing a pylon turn, a basic maneuver in which the airplane is flown in a perfect circle, keeping a point on the ground in the absolute center of the turn. But now, there was physical connection between the aircraft and the ground. The young officer's imagination took over, and in his mind's eye, he pictured the rope as the path of a bullet fired from the airplane. If a gun, mounted on the side of a circling airplane, could be aimed at the center of the circle, the bullet would strike the exact center of the circle each and every time, regardless of the relative position of the airplane in its orbit.

How this epiphany made its way to the research and development folks in the air force is still a mystery. But it started a revolution that forever changed the world of aerial warfare.

CHAPTER 2

✦

THE AIRFRAMES

E very story has its basis in facts and, in this case, technical merit. Before the story can be told, the reader needs some background on the technology of the aircraft and supporting onboard systems.

The C-47 became the first test bed for a new concept called the fixed-wing gunship. First produced in the 1930s, the two-engine transport saw service as the C-47 in its military role and the DC-3 as a civilian airliner. Over sixteen thousand of these aircraft were built in the thirties and forties. Several hundred are still in service around the world. For the gunship configuration, three SUU-11/A minigun pods were installed on the left side of the aircraft, and the AC-47 "*Spooky*" was born. Later versions saw the installation of the MXU-470/A minigun module. The major difference between the two systems is that the SUU-11/A was a long, pod-like configuration designed and mounted on wing stations of fighter-sized aircraft. The MXU-470/A utilized a more vertical configuration, in which the ammo supply was stored beneath the gun rather than behind it. It kind of resembles a large cigar sitting on top of a coffee can. This freed about two to three feet of space inside the cargo compartment, which was critical, given the rather small dimensions of a C-47. Additionally, the MXU-470/A provided two thousand rounds of ammunition as opposed to the fifteen hundred rounds carried in the SUU-11/A. The MXU-470/A also featured a fire rate select switch that allowed two thousand– or four thousand–round-per-minute bursts. The MXU-470 also incorporated an electric feed system, which allowed fast in-flight reloading. The SUU-11/A was equipped with a manual hand crank and took a great deal longer to reload. The pilot had a WWII fighter optical gun sight mounted in his left window that was bore-sighted to the firing line of the guns. During a fire mission, the pilot would begin a pylon turn and place the illuminated dot (the pipper) on the intended target. If all three guns were configured for their maximum rate of fire, a press of the trigger button sent up to eighteen thousand rounds a minute of 7.62mm ammo toward the target. The AC-47 Spooky became the airborne weapon of choice for troops in contact, or TIC, missions. If a hamlet, firebase, or just plain grunts came under fire by enemy troops, Spooky would roll in, and the entire situation would be reversed in an instant. During the entire length of the conflict, not a single engagement of this type was ever lost to the enemy if the AC-47 was called in.

In Laos, there was a network of roads, jungle paths and trails, rivers, streams, and tunnels the North Vietnamese would use secretly to move troops, armaments, and supplies to the south. This network was commonly referred to as the Ho Chi Minh Trail. The United States and its allies knew of the trail and sent in everything from fighter-bombers to B-52s to attack it with little or no impact. Part of the reason for this failure was that it's very difficult to see through jungle canopy at all, much less place a bomb onto a truck when traveling at several hundred miles an hour. The other issue was that these types of aircraft burn a significant amount of fuel in a short period. That being the case, their loiter time was severely curtailed. Adding to the dilemma was that this type of strike ultimately had a positive impact for the enemy. The enormous number of large bombs used in the endeavor created instant crushed stone and gravel pits. The enemy troops no longer needed to bring in larger excavation equipment needed for constant road construction and repair.

Military planners knew that they needed something smaller, slower, and more accurate than the fast movers and heavy bombers it had employed up to that time. The AC-47 filled the bill, but its weaponry simply wasn't heavy enough to deal with large vehicles and road equipment. The minigun uses a 7.62mm rifle cartridge that can decimate an army of personnel. But it does little more than destructive rust removal on a five-thousand-pound truck or road grader. Something else had to be found. Enter the Hercules.

The C-130 is an amazing, if not humble, aircraft. In its designed state, it has the ability to haul large amounts of heavy cargo in and out of everything from a standard airport runway to an unimproved short dirt strip in the middle of nowhere. Its four turboprop engines utilize the same jet fuel as the fast movers but at a consumption rate well below that of its high-speed counterparts. With its heavy lift capability, it had the potential of mounting heavier weapons than the AC-47, and this is precisely what it did. The program was called Gunship II, and the original designs saw four 20 mm Vulcan canons and four miniguns installed. Like the minigun, the Vulcan was a six-barreled Gatling design. But that's where the similarity ended. While the minigun used rifle ammunition, the Vulcan utilized 20 mm ammo with high explosive (and other) projectiles. A well-placed hit on a vehicle by one of these rounds will cause the vehicle to become totally disabled, destroyed, or even explode. The use of Vulcans in the AC-130 was initially looked on favorably. Exploding and incendiary projectiles were a huge improvement. Additionally, the use of this particular gun allowed better standoff capability than was seen with the AC-47. Spooky operated at fifteen hundred feet. Although it did a superb job for what it was designed, it simply wasn't suited for an arena that bristled with heavy antiaircraft weapons. The first Spectres flew at seventy-five hundred feet of altitude, which provided a bit more time and distance to react if they came under attack. But this was eventually shown to be wishful thinking, as two of these variants were lost to ground fire in 1969 and 1970. The AC-130 was proving to be a very valuable asset, and the air force wished to keep them. They just needed to come up with a better way to keep them safe. This was accomplished in late 1970 when "Surprise Package" was unveiled. Spectre could always see in the dark, but now it did so more effectively, and it had bigger teeth. Two of the miniguns and two of the Vulcans were replaced by two 40 mm Bofors canons. The Bofors was a Swedish-designed, pre-WWII weapon that was originally intended as an antiaircraft gun. And, like the 20 mm, the 40 mm rounds came in several variants that included high explosive, armor piercing, incendiary, and even tracer types. These guns were quite prolific in their day, and thousands were produced. The army had the air-cooled version, and the navy used a water-cooled type. Both are commonly seen in WWII newsreels and action movies. The air-cooled army version was selected for the gunship. Both were mounted just forward of the left paratroop door. There was only one negative issue with the Bofors: they could not be fired simultaneously, as they would quite literally rip out the floor. However, that issue was never really a problem, as one of these fire breathers was more than enough to take out any vehicle that might be found on the trail. They were even known to take out enemy tanks with just one or two rounds.

The other major change included in Surprise Package was the upgrade and additions to the electronic sensors. A low light level TV (LLTV) was installed to replace the NOD (night observation device). The NOD was essentially a manually operated, large trainable starlight scope mounted in the crew-entry door. Its position rates were fed into the fire control computer. It was good but had limitations, primary of which was the need for lighting provided by the moon and stars. The LLTV, on the other hand, was helped by a 2 kW infrared (IR) light mounted near the cargo door that was slaved to the position of the TV. With an IR filter attached, the light couldn't be seen on the ground, but it tremendously improved the ability of the TV to see things on the ground with increased clarity. The LLTV generally became the primary sensor during an attack. It had a wide-angle capability, which was used to scan a large area of ground to detect targets. On detection, it would switch to the narrow-angle mode for the attack. Next was the IR, or infrared, sensor. This device picked up and displayed the heat given off by vehicle engines and even people. There was a Stone Age variant on the original gunship, but it was replaced by a unit that was so effective it allowed one to see the drivers run from their trucks when under attack. The bad news is that, later, we could see drivers were chained to their steering wheels to prevent them from running away. We liked to think of ourselves as honorable warriors, but that always bummed us out. The next electronic goody was the BC, or Black Crow. It derived that name because it was operated by an electronic warfare officer, usually out of the Strategic Air Command. Since the dawn of airborne electronic countermeasures, the symbol for the operator was the black crow. The BC was a technical marvel that had its roots in AM car radios. At least that's the way I saw it. Anyone who ever rode in a car in the fifties and sixties with just an AM radio will remember what happened every time you drove under high-tension lines. The music would be replaced by very loud static that was rather annoying caused by electrons jumping off the high voltage wires. The car's antenna would catch these electrons and "play" them on the radio for us. We also remember that there were condensers in the ignition systems that were used to prevent the same static from our own vehicle's engine from jamming our radios. The vehicles supplied to North Vietnam didn't have these condensers; nor were their ignition systems shielded. The BC was a car radio that knew somebody. In other words, it had a directional antenna and circuitry that allowed the operator to detect vehicles twenty miles away from ignition noise and point directly at the source. About 50 percent of the time, it was the BC that found the targets first. The only failing of the BC sensor was that it was useless against diesel-powered vehicles. Fortunately, the majority of vehicles used on the Ho Chi Minh Trail were gasoline powered. This brings us to the final feature of the sensors: Each was able to "slave" to the others at the press of a button. If the BC found a "mover" (an underway vehicle), the other two sensors would simply slave to the BC, and their sensors would be looking at the same place.

The next bit of magic was the pilot's gun sight. It was a heads-up display (HUD). It was part rifle scope and part pinball machine. Among other bits of data being shown in this device, two reticles—or crosshairs—

were displayed in the HUD. One was called the "fixed" reticle. It was a stationary electronic representation of the gun line. The other was the "moving" reticle. It moved around the confines of the HUD and was a representation of where the sensor was looking, after having been modified by the computer with airspeed, altitude, wind direction, and so on. The pilot flew the airplane is such a way as to align, or "superimpose," the moving reticle over the fixed one. After the guns were electrically armed by the gunners and flight engineer at their respective stations, the pilot pressed a button on his yoke (steering wheel), and the selected gun(s) would fire. If the guns were properly bore sighted, and the fire control computer working, the target on the ground would simply "go away," usually in a burst of explosion and flame.

At the end of hostilities, the North Vietnamese admitted that the two things they feared the most during the conflict were the B-52 Stratofortress and the AC-130 Spectre. Their problem with a B-52 strike is obvious. But their concern about the gunship was a little different. They could hear a turbo prop overhead and then their vehicles and equipment would very accurately be destroyed. The B-52 was like a street brawler. One could see it coming and knew the results would be devastating. The gunship, however, was like an invisible surgeon that removed critical body parts before you could react.

A bit of trivia:

During a B-52 (Arc Light) strike, 108 500-pound bombs would be released when the bomber was configured for its maximum load. Given the amount of time for this to occur (ten seconds or more) and the distance a B-52 can travel at 500 miles per hour during that time, the length of the string of bombs would be on the order of several city blocks. With luck, a few of these bombs *may* hit the intended target.

When everything in the gunship is aligned and in perfect working order, the accuracy of the AC-130 at ground level is plus or minus ten feet from ten thousand feet of altitude. In layman's terms, this means that an unattached garage, twenty feet from a house, could be attacked and destroyed with very little, or no collateral damage to the house. Pretty good specs for a cobbled-together weapons platform.

CHAPTER 3

✪

THE AIR FORCE, THE GUNSHIP, AND ME

The year is 1967. We had been living in a small town in eastern Pennsylvania at the fringe of the Pennsylvania Dutch country. My mom had remarried in 1965 to a man from Philly who owned a manufacturing company in Ontario, Canada. They agreed that we wouldn't move there until I finished my senior year in high school.

We eventually moved to Ontario in the summer of 1966. I took a year of high school up there, as they had a Grade 13 in those days. Although part of the high school system, Grade 13 was equivalent to a freshman year of college. That meant that if you went to college there, you would start in your sophomore year. Everyone in my family had gone to college, and I was expected to attend. Being a lazy student, I let down the family tradition and elected not to go. This was the time of draft dodgers and young men fleeing to Canada. Perhaps I'm too straight and too patriotic, but the term "draft dodger" was a label I didn't take kindly to. So, in December of that year, I traveled to Buffalo and enlisted in the US Air Force. From there, it was off to San Antonio, Texas, and Lackland Air Force Base for basic training.

My air force aptitude test showed I had a penchant for mechanical and technical things. One day, several of us with that aptitude score were summoned to a large building on Lackland referred to as the Green Monster. There, the personnel folks assisted in determining what career field is best suited for each person. We sat in a room with a large chalkboard. In front of the board was a cardstock sign planted on an easel. Printed on this sign were the career fields that were available to us based on our scores. In our case, there were about five fields from which we could choose. The one I remember (and sometimes regret) the most for not taking was refrigeration and air conditioning. That falls under the category of, "If I'd known then what I know now." As I read through the remaining choices, one stuck out. I immediately asked the specialist what "weapons and munitions" was. He answered that it entailed the building, loading, testing, and maintenance of aircraft bombs, rockets, missiles, and guns. I've always loved airplanes and have had firearms since I was eight years old, so that was for me. So, off I went to Denver, Colorado, and Lowry Air Force Base for tech school. Because I scored fairly high on my tests, I was sent to the Tactical Air Command (TAC) portion of the school, which was the longest at eighteen weeks. The other two major command schools were Strategic Air Command (SAC), which employed bombers, and Aerospace Defense Command (ADC), which used interceptors. They were shorter only because there weren't as many aircraft and weapon types to learn as there were in TAC. I was obviously pretty proud of myself at this "honor" and studied hard for the next few months. The curriculum included study of F-4s, F-105s, F-100s; there was one of each in the mysterious hangar they called Black Shack. There was even a mockup of the brand-new F-111. The Black Shack and its contents were classified enough that anyone who needed access to that building had to have the initial portion of his security clearance completed before being allowed in. With the exception of intercontinental ballistic missiles (ICBMs) and the larger thermonuclear weapons carried by bombers, I was given the opportunity to "play" with nearly everything in the US arsenal that could be carried, dropped, fired, or launched by any type of fighter aircraft in the inventory. In this line of work, snap, crackle, and pop meant a lot more than breakfast cereal. I was in heaven. I did very well in tech school and got high marks for my efforts. But then, the bottom dropped out. In June of 1967, I graduated tech school and got my first assignment: Wurtsmith Air Force Base, Michigan. Although my tech school had trained me in the TAC side of the house, I was to work on B-52s, which were a SAC asset. I complained about this to anyone who would listen, as I had no SAC training. However, my complaints fell on deaf ears, and I was on my way to the Upper Midwest. There, I was immediately struck by the only similarity between a B-52 and a fighter: it flies and makes a big noise and lots of fire when it does its job. Naturally, load training for me took forever, and I wasn't very popular with the guys who preceded me there. In their day, one went to tech school and learned *all* the aircraft. The curriculum had not yet been segregated into major commands and aircraft types. They simply could not comprehend the aspect of being trained in only one type. I was made to feel like Typhoid Mary. Fortunately for me, my time in Michigan was rather short lived. Within three months of arriving, I had orders to Okinawa to load conventional bombs on B-52s bound for 'Nam. First, however, I had to go back to Denver for a month of temporary duty to learn how to load conventional (iron) bombs, instead of nukes, on a B-52.

As of November of 1968, I had been assigned to four bases, was on my way to my fifth, and I hadn't even been on active duty a year yet. I've known people who spent nearly their entire career at one base, although that was quite rare.

By the time I returned to the States in March of 1970, I felt as if I'd lost part of my life. The years 1968, 1969, and 1970 were the most tumultuous years in the country, and I felt as if I'd missed them. There was a revolution in music, fashion, and trends, and nearly an armed revolution in our country due to the political environment of the time. Granted, we got the new music over there, and we had a plethora of news from every type of media available at the time. But, it just wasn't the same as being there.

I was assigned to Castle AFB, California. It's located in the middle of the San Joaquin Valley, about sixty miles north of Fresno. And, once again, I'm at the mercy of B-52s. I was beginning to forget what a fighter looked like, much less how to load weapons on one and perform tests on their electronic equipment. Okinawa can tend to be pretty warm, except when a typhoon comes by. But the San Joaquin Valley is absolutely brutal during the summer months. The temperature on the flight line can reach 110 degrees. The interiors of the B-52s parked on that flight line occasionally reached 145 degrees or more. If you have been tasked to perform a critical circuits maintenance check (CCMC), you'll spend an average of an hour and a half doing your Hansel-and-Gretel-in-the-oven impression, pausing several times to empty the sweat from the ear cups of your headset. I figured that, since I was a motorcycle rider, I was at least in a good, year-round riding climate. This, too, proved to be a myth. There were times when it was so hot the clutch and front brake levers on my bike were too hot to touch. Many were the times when I had to wait 'til 7 p.m. or later just to enjoy a short cruise after work. I began to think that I'd done something horrible in a previous life to be tormented like this by B-52s and temperatures suited only to vulcanizing rubber.

But, one day I was delivered. I noticed an article in the local base newspaper that the rank requirement for gunship gunners had been reduced. The gunners on a fixed-wing gunship held the same specialty code (or MOS) as a weapons and munitions person and simply had an A added to the beginning of the code, which simply describes an airborne specialty. Apparently, they were in need of a lot more folks, and I looked into it. Ultimately, I volunteered and was accepted, along with Joel, another bomb loader with whom I was stationed. This is when my air force career finally came to fruition, at least as I saw it.

CHAPTER 4

✪

THE TRAINING AND THE CREWS

Before actually flying combat sorties in Southeast Asia, one must endure loads of training that entails no fewer than three temporary duty assignments, or TDYs. The first of these assignments was flight training at Lockbourne AFB in Ohio. (Today, the base is called Rickenbacker Field and belongs to the Air National Guard). This is where I got my first look at the AC-130A. Prior to this point, I had seen standard cargo C-130 Hercules, or Herkey Birds, just about everywhere. We affectionately referred to them as "Plain Janes" or "trash haulers." Actually, we affectionately called every transport/cargo airplane a trash hauler, so we weren't just picking on the Herky Bird. Our first look at the gunship version was more than slightly amazing. Instead of the usual camouflage paint job, this thing was pitch-black except for the top, which retained the camo appearance. This was to ensure that an enemy aircraft above the gunship would have difficulty seeing it against the background of the ground. Other things stuck out as well. The most prolific C-130 variant that most of us were used to seeing during that time was the E-Model, which sported four-bladed props with rounded tips on its turboprop engines. But this was an A-Model, which was produced with longer, three-bladed props with squared tips. Another difference was that the E-Model had external fuel tanks located between the engines on each wing. The A-Model's tanks were positioned outboard of the outer engines. Regardless of the difference in appearance, this thing looked menacing and dangerous. I immediately fell in love with it!

The crew compliment of an AC-130 is a bit different from most other combat aircraft as well. We had a pilot, copilot, navigator (nav), and flight engineer. This was a typical compliment for most airlift type airplanes, minus the loadmaster. There was a booth (room) in the center of the cargo deck. Its dimensions were about ten by twenty feet. This is where our team of sensor operators worked. Initially, the nav, on the flight deck, acted as the fire control officer (FCO), but as the airplane and mission evolved, he was later augmented by an additional position in the booth with the designation of FCO.

The next man was the Illuminator Operator (IO). The initial design of the AC-130 had an incredibly powerful spotlight called the Illuminator, mounted on the loading ramp, and this was operated by the IO. The Illuminator's life was a short one and was eventually replaced by a flare launcher, which was also operated by the IO. The flares were the MK24. The flare launcher held about twenty flares, which were launched by pneumatic pressure. The MK24 was about three feet long and about six inches in diameter. When launched, they would ignite and a parachute would deploy, slowing their descent. At several million candlepower, they had the ability to illuminate a huge hunk of ground. That was the good news. The bad news was that they could also illuminate us, giving away our position to the antiaircraft gunners that were all over the trail. For obvious reasons, we only used them when absolutely necessary. The IO was also equipped with the MK 6 flare. The MK 6 is a piece of navy equipment that had wonderful properties we could exploit. It was essentially a two-foot long, waterproof piece of four-by-four lumber with tiny red and white phosphorous fillers. One was used to ignite the wood immediately on activation, and the other would support combustion over a period of time to allow the wood to sustain its own burning. If launched during daylight, the smoke provided a point of reference on the ground or in the water. At night, the visible flame from the flare provided the reference.

The primary role of the IO, and the way he accomplished it, set him apart from every other crew position. He would don his parachute harness, sans the parachute. On the ceiling of the airplane, an inertia reel was mounted. Its mechanical action is similar to the work light used by auto mechanics but with one major difference. If one pulled slowly, the braided steel cable would play out to any length. Pulled on sharply, the cable would lock. The cable of the inertia reel was hooked to a loop on the IO's parachute harness. He needed this rig, as his duty called for him to lie on his belly with the upper half of his body outside the airplane. On the AC-130, the loading ramp was up, but the loading door was open. His job was to search for any antiaircraft artillery (AAA or Triple A) or surface to air missiles, while simultaneously alerting the crew to these threats and calling for evasive maneuvers when required. The inertia reel saved more than a couple IOs. Some evasive maneuvers caused the airplane to experience negative Gs. When this happened, the IO would literally float off the ramp. If he were lucky, part of the airplane would still be under him when positive Gs were encountered once again. Occasionally, the only thing under an IO when this happened was open air. Therein lies the secret of having a locking inertia reel attached to his parachute harness. One such incident will be highlighted later in the story.

The last group of crew members was the gunners. We were called gunners for practicality reasons. Our technical title was airborne weapons technician. We were the jacks-of-all-trades on the crew. There were five of us, and we did a different job each night. Two gunners were needed to man the Bofors: one to pass the ammo from its storage container and one to stuff the four-round clips into the gun. Gunner #3 would man the 20 mms, usually referred to as the "front guns." Most of his duties entailed cleaning up the brass as the gun fired. And at twenty-five hundred rounds a minute, a great deal of brass and links accumulated very quickly. As with the Bofors crew, the front gunner had to be ready to intervene at a moment's notice if a gun stopped working. This happened fairly regularly, and that's where the intense training comes into play. No lighting was permitted on the gunship. Flying at a relatively low altitude, at a very slow airspeed, was risky enough. It wasn't necessary to add to the hazard by shining lights that, even from the inside of the aircraft, could be seen from the ground. With the exception of a small, handheld NiCad flashlight with a red filter, all the work was done to the guns in total darkness. That work reminded me of the old movies, in which a trainee was required to field strip his weapon blindfolded. When push came to shove, that's where we "made our money." The #4 gunner was the "aisle man." This name came from the rather narrow aisle created when the booth was installed, leaving about a three-foot corridor between the booth and the left wheel well. The #4 man would wander the aisle as a "spare" to assist when necessary the front or rear gunners. The miniguns were also located in that area, and he was responsible for them if they were used. They never were. The altitude required for their use was *way* too low, and we simply didn't go down there. Those guns were eventually removed due to inactivity but reinstalled several years later on upgraded models. The last gunner, #5, didn't act in the literal capacity of a gunner at all. Due to an aircraft design anomaly only associated with the gunship and not the cargo version, the IO had a blind spot on the right side of the aircraft, meaning he was unable to see ground fire while the aircraft was in a pylon turn to the left. On nearly every C-130 variant, there's an emergency escape hatch located in the right fuselage, directly aft of the propeller line and just forward of the right wheel well. On the AC-130, the hatch door was removed and a platform installed onto the floor. A seat was attached to this platform and positioned in such a way as to allow the occupant to sit at the hatch and lean out if necessary. This crew position was referred to as the right scanner. The #5 gunner would position himself there and add an extra set of eyes into the IO's blind spot. Manning that position reminded me of a dog with its head out the window of a moving automobile.

The classroom studies were interesting enough, but I wanted to fly in this mean-looking bugger. Our first mission was strictly an orientation flight for the entire crew. Initially, it was almost hard to remember we were in a combat airplane. Later on, however, we didn't have that problem. We practiced pylon turns and evasive maneuvers that made me think we were shooting an episode of *Voyage to the Bottom of the Sea*, in which the submarine tilts violently from left to right, causing the crewmen to behave as clappers in a bell. The only difference was that we didn't have sparks and flames shooting out of the electrical panels, and there was no dramatic music playing in the background. But, like all the other gunners, I was waiting for our first live-fire mission. When it became our time, we flew over Lake Erie. The IO dropped an MK 6 flare into the water. The flare represented a target, and we flew a pylon turn around it, firing at it when all the computer ducks were lined up and it allowed the firing voltage to reach the gun. Our favorite gun during the training flights was the Bofors. We used tracer ammo for it in order for all the players to see and get a feel for what happens during an attack. There was a very unusual optical illusion associated with firing the Bofors. As the round left the barrel and the tracer ignited, its forward (horizontal) speed would bleed off, and the airplane would continue forward. The projectile seemed to arc back behind the airplane and then arc forward again to impact the target. One would expect to see a red dot leave the gun and stay in the same horizontal position of the aircraft, not take a crescent shaped path to the surface. As the Bofors fired, the expended round ejected out the back of the gun and was deflected into a fifty-five-gallon drum that was held in place by a ratcheting tie-down strap.

The 20 mm Vulcans were a whole other horse. They didn't use tracer, both could be fired at the same time, and they made a noise like nothing ever heard before. During our time at tech school in Denver, we witnessed twenty-five rounds fired from a Vulcan. But the gun was on the other side of a wall with a thick glass window. The full twenty-five rounds used for the demo were eaten up in a quarter second. By the time it was over, we were still waiting for it to happen. But when in an airplane, with these things just a few feet away, the sound stays with one for life. Although both 20s could be fired simultaneously, we rarely did. The obvious reason was it used up ammo at an accelerated rate. The other reason was that the recoil was so intense firing both guns at the same time pushed the aircraft sideways and nearly out of the orbit. And because of the accuracy of the system and the inability to carry more than a few thousand rounds of ammunition, the gun wasn't fired at its optimal rate of six thousand rounds per minute. We fired at twenty-five hundred rounds per minute, but the noise was still shocking. Trying to describe or imitate that sound to someone who has never heard it is virtually impossible. As kids playing war, all of us were able to simulate the rat-atta-tat of a machine gun. But how would we simulate the noise of a fifty-foot elephant with intestinal gas and a megaphone? And watching the ammo feed from the can to the gun was also something to behold. When we watched the old war movies, we saw each round of belted ammunition being fed into the machine gun. It was fairly fast, but we could still make out the individual rounds. But, trying to watch the 20 mm ammo running through the feed chute with the gun firing is akin to attempting to read the manufacturer's name on a fan belt with the engine running. The feed unit on the Vulcan also provides an exit chute for its brass as it's expended. Here's where the system on a gunship gets more "Rube Goldberg." Below the exit chute, the sheet metal folks fabricated a metal ramp that directed the spent cases away from the gun and onto the floor of the airplane. However, this portion of the floor had a box built into it. In essence, it was a simple structure that was four one-foot high walls that contained the brass as it slid down the sheet metal ramp. Further inspection of this portion of the airplane reveals several neatly stacked and folded military duffel bags and a coal shovel. When a break in the action occurred, or the brass box got too full, the gunner assigned to the front guns was tasked to cleaning up the brass. He grabbed the coal shovel, and the aisle man held open the duffel bag. The brass from all the guns was retained for military reasons. The North Vietnamese obviously didn't have the industrial might of the United States and coveted anything we threw away. For example, they would dig out the high explosives from our bombs that failed to detonate and make antipersonnel weapons and booby traps from it. Large brass casings were also very valuable to them. They could be melted down and recast to make new ammunition. One of the urban legends of the time told of the bad guys who would take our 40 mm brass and neck it down to be reused as 37 mm, the most prolific antiaircraft weapons in Southeast Asia, and fired back at us. The legend also held that our 20 mm brass would be necked up to be reloaded as 23 mm, the bane of small and low-flying US aircraft. The ZSU-23/4 Shilka was a self-propelled, radar guided, four-barreled antiaircraft weapon that could put out nearly four thousand rounds a minute at an unsuspecting low flyer. Its smaller brother, the ZSU-23/2, was a two-barreled version used by North Vietnamese field units. Many a forward air controller (FAC) and fast-moving fighter were lost to these systems.

The following AC-130As were severely damaged by enemy fire during my year at Ubon. The list doesn't not include the multitude of airplanes that suffered minor airburst shrapnel hits.

Tail #630, *Azreal*—Struck in the horizontal stabilizer by, fortunately, a 57 mm antiaircraft shell. I use the word "fortunately," because a 57 mm travels much faster than a 37 mm. The round pierced the stabilizer, but its speed was fast enough so that the detonation occurred above the stabilizer, soaking up most of the shrapnel. Had it been 37 mm, the round would have detonated immediately on impact, most likely killing or severely wounding the IO lying on his belly, just a few feet below. As it was, the IO suffered no injury whatsoever.

Tail #129, The *First Lady*—Direct hit just aft of the nose gear wheel well. The story of this encounter will be told in its own chapter.

Tail #044, *Prometheus*—This aircraft did, in fact, suffer incredibly severe damage during my stay in Thailand—however, not from enemy fire. Like the *First Lady*, its story is told in detail in another section of the book.

CHAPTER 5

✪

THE FIRST SURVIVAL SCHOOL

The next phase of my training was air force survival school at Fairchild AFB, in Washington. This was referred to as "general" survival, as it encompassed all aspects of survival, rather than one specific type we'd be exposed to later. As with nearly all of the AF schools, this one was segregated into two parts: classroom and field. Even the classroom portion diverged into two parts. The indoor portion was interesting but mundane, except for the portion that dealt with understanding communist doctrine as it applied to warfare. I don't recall too much of what was discussed with the exception of the comments by one of our more colorful instructors. He constantly referred to our adversaries as, "Those pinko, pinko commie bastards"!

Next came the instruction on basic parachute use. In the first portion, we learned how to fall properly when hitting the ground. It was called the parachute landing fall (PLF). We renamed it PFL: poor f-ing legs. Striking Mother Earth at fifteen to twenty miles per hour was *not* our idea of a good time. We practiced our five-point landings in the gymnasium, jumping off of stepladders or other platforms onto those smelly, gray gym mats. We looked and felt like idiots, but it had its purpose.

The next part of parachute training was water landing. For this, we went to the pool. A thirty-foot tower was erected at one end. On top of the tower was a ramplike affair that had an aircraft seat with bogey wheels on the bottom. It was set up like a roller-coaster car. It was placed on rails that pointed downward, toward the water, and held in place by a single large, removable pin. Above the car, an overhead cable and pulley setup ran the length of the pool, and the parachute harness was attached to it. One sits in the seat, dons the parachute harness, and the seat is released. At the bottom end of the rails, a cam-shaped protrusion caused the car to stop abruptly and tilted it forward, causing the occupant to be unceremoniously ejected into thin air whether he wants to or not. It doesn't matter how strong we are or how much adrenaline is pumping. We are not staying in that seat.

One free falls several feet, until a lanyard attached to the pulley jerks the person to a stop. This is to simulate the "opening shock" of the chute. One dangles for several more seconds before the lanyard is released. The slide down the cable and ultimate submersion into the pool simulates descending with wind and ending with a water landing.

One of the scarier aspects of a water landing occurs when there is no wind. In this instance, the chute comes down directly above the head, rather than in front or behind. When this happens, one finds himself trapped in the water under a twenty-nine-foot canopy. As expected, some of the students became panic-stricken by this and freaked out. Fortunately, there were several instructors positioned in the water for rescue if it became necessary. The technique used to free oneself is rather simple. To keep from becoming disoriented, locate one of the radiating cords sewn into the canopy and follow it to the edge, while simultaneously pushing up on the canopy to provide an air pocket. While unkind, I have to admit to having a giggle at the bodybuilders and linebacker types who could not get out from under their canopy and turned into scared little boys. It took one of them about a half hour to regain his composure. He'd become Billy Bad Ass again, until he was threatened with a return to the parachute pool. He behaved for the remainder of the course. There's an old adage that goes, "Anticipation of death is worse than death itself." In his case, replace the word "death" with "parachute pool," and you get the picture.

The second phase of the training was the obstacle course. We were led outside to an area bordering the woods. It began by introducing us to the different types of rescue flares with which we'd need to become familiar. One was the MK-13. A two-ended device, it had the same dimensions as a half of a paper towel tube. It offered a bright flare for nighttime use, and activating the other end produces a thick red smoke for daytime use. An interesting addition to this flare was that it had little bumps on the plastic protective end cap and around the circumference of the night end of the tube. Otherwise, in pure darkness, it would be difficult to determine which end was which.

The bumps were strictly there as a reminder and prevented a few folks from wasting their smoke flare. This flare was fine if floating on the water in a raft or our Mae West. But it was not a great idea when trying to hide from the bad guys. The exception would be when the search and rescue (SAR) folks were on the radio with us and instructed us to use it. There were two other devices that could be called flare guns. The first, and older, type, shot red stars into the air, like a Roman candle. This is great if the SAR guys were looking for you and needed a point of reference, *and* providing you were in fairly flat, mostly open country. The problem with this unit was that the stars didn't reach a very high altitude and didn't have the power to punch through the triple canopy rain forest that's so prevalent in Southeast Asia. Enter the gyro jet. This was a similar-looking flare gun but with a twist in the operation. The first gun had a trigger that was pulled back with a thumb and then released. The flare cartridge was screwed into the tube, and when fired, a small explosive charge propelled the stars out of the cartridge and into the air. The gyro jet's cartridge was pressed into the tube, and when fired, the primer ignited rocket propellant that was jetted out of two angled nozzles in the rear of the cartridge. The cartridge had the power to rise to an altitude of fifteen hundred feet and penetrate tree branches along the way. We got a chance to fire each of these.

As we were led into this field in late afternoon, darkness began to fall. This wasn't coincidental. Now it was time for the obstacle course. The course was a half-mile long, L-shaped affair loaded with patrols, trip wires, and booby traps. There was a rule that if someone nearby trips a flare or other device, you wouldn't be tagged if you kept perfectly still. The tagged person is considered captured and leaves the course. Even if you successfully traverse the entire length of the course, you suffer the same fate as the captured guy by simple default: you leave the course and surrender. An OD laundry bag is placed over the head and acts like a blindfold. I just wish they'd have washed mine before they slipped it over my head. I won't describe the odor I encountered as I promised my pastor I wouldn't use those words. Smelly bag notwithstanding, the next twenty-four to seventy-two hours tested my mettle and gave me a lot of insight into my own psyche, adaptability and morality. Depending on mental state, it can be a test of character or cowardice.

After all the participants have finished the obstacle course, "surrendered," and had their heads bagged, we were led off to the prison camp. This is where we got our first taste of what an enemy might do to disorient us and get us totally confused about cardinal headings. Prior to being "laundry bagged" the camp was visible and only about one hundred yards away. But, when we were led away hand to shoulder, we could tell we were heading in a direction other than where we had seen the camp. The hundred-yard walk took about six hundred yards and several ninety-degree turns to get there. We were taken into igloos, previously used as weapons storage, and placed in a box that was 4 × 4 × 6 feet. We were given an empty, three-pound coffee can and told it was our latrine. Additionally, we were to remain standing at attention, with our hoods on, at all times. We were kept in the boxes for a day, and the guards would sneak up and fling the door open without notice. You had better be found standing, awake, and with hood on. There were small openings at the bottom of the door, where they'd pass in food and water.

After release from our boxes, we were let loose into the main prison compound. The compound was set up to resemble the type of facility one might encounter in Southeast Asia. There was one noticeable difference, however. This was November in Washington State. The temperatures at night fell below freezing, and the stay in these conditions was not pleasant. During our indoor classroom study, we were advised to attempt to smuggle foodstuffs into the camp. Part of the reason was that we couldn't expect decent rations while in captivity. But, the major reason was to provide nutrition to those who were already imprisoned and probably malnourished. Obviously, the latter wouldn't be true in our case, but this was training for the real thing, and we got the impression that we wouldn't be given very substantial food in the camp. This proved to be sadly true on the first night, when we were given firewood, a large cast iron pot, and some uncooked rice. We began cooking the rice and had someone go out and collect whatever food was smuggled in. These were added to the boiling rice, and the most disgusting-looking gruel was produced. It consisted mainly of jerky, Slim Jims, pemmican, corn chips, and several other snack foods. Since we had not eaten in over twenty-four hours and the temps were hovering around thirty degrees, that gruel was some of the best tasting stuff I'd ever eaten.

The camp was set up with the traditional communist flair: marching to and from everywhere, greeting any of the guards with the words, "Bycon, Comrade," and attending communist indoctrination classes. The classes were stereotypical in the extreme. We were informed that we were all pawns of a corrupt government and that we all worked for Wall Street. The list goes on and on, but one can use his imagination for the rest.

The camp commandant was a little fellow named Ivan. He had a very authentic-sounding accent that fell somewhere between Russian and Bela Lugosi's Dracula. He also possessed an attitude that let you know he was in charge. He and the guards wore black uniforms with red stars. They really looked the part, and by day two, it would be easy to start to disbelieve reality and think one was being held by some really nasty bad guys. They even had a North Vietnamese flag hoisted atop the flagpole. It was the most god-awful sight in the entire camp.

By the third day, we were all pretty subdued but elated by knowing we would be released that morning. As usual, we woke up and had to acknowledge the hated flag. Then we were called into formation and began marching toward the gate and freedom. About twenty yards shy of the gate, Ivan appeared and stopped us. In his thick Russian accent, he began a diatribe that caused the entire formation to collectively moan in frustration and disbelief. He told us that we were poor students and didn't learn a thing. By the time he was nearly finished, he told us that we weren't fit to leave and that we would have to stay another day or two, until we were thoroughly trained. With this revelation, there was a another collective moan from the assembled students. He barked out an about-face, and we turned. The sight that met us was enough to make even the toughest man weak in the knees. The North Vietnamese flag had been replaced with the American flag, and the National Anthem began playing. There wasn't a dry eye anywhere, and all the camp guards saluted us as we left the compound. If you weren't a patriot when you entered the camp, you certainly were when you left. The days in the compound was as horrific a time as I've ever spent in my life. But, the lessons learned there were most likely the most important, lifesaving lessons a person about to go into combat could get. A huge, "Atta-boy," for Ivan, his staff, and the staff of the entire school.

A bit of trivia: We found out later that Ivan came by his acting, and accent, honestly. We commented to a senior instructor how well we thought Ivan portrayed his role and how authentic the accent was. We jokingly referred to the "school" Ivan must have attended in order to gain so much insight. It was then we were informed that he had graduated from the school of hard knocks. Ivan was actually Polish and grew up during WWII. When he was still quite young, he and his family were arrested and brutalized by the Nazis. After the war, he met the same fate at the hands of the KGB (then NKVD), during the Soviet occupation of Eastern Europe.

Part two of the school was known as the Trek. Anyone familiar with most educational curriculums knows that students start with the theory and then move to the lab, where what was learned in the classroom is put into practice. The Trek was the lab. We were stuffed into the traditional blue air force buses and shipped to a site in the boonies, about sixty miles north of the base. If any community name gives credence to a wilderness area, the town of Usk, Washington, was it. Even then, the Trek area was another few miles outside of Usk.

We were eventually dropped off in a clearing after a kidney-jolting ride on an unimproved logging road. In the clearing, we were given the rules and instructions for conducting this phase of the training. One of the more interesting facts was that the air force had an agreement with the state DEC, in which each instructor was given a permit that allowed his team of students to take one deer during the outing. This sounded good, but when all one had was a folding survival knife and some snare wire, such a feat seemed unlikely.

Our team was comprised of three or four officers and two enlisted. I was a buck sergeant at the time, and the other enlisted person was a technical sergeant. One of the officers in our group was a young second lieutenant from India. No one could pronounce his name, so we called him Teddy, a phonetic derivation of his real name. Teddy was a pleasant, likable, young navigator, who carried a knife from home. It was about seven inches long and looked like something out of *Arabian Nights*. It was curved into a crescent shape and had a V-notch at the end of the blade, nearest the handle. We inquired into the reason for the notch. To our horror, he explained that when one sneaks up behind an enemy and slits his throat, the notch grabs the jugular vein and rips it out. Needless to say, everyone planned to be very nice to Teddy for the remainder of the Trek. That is, until the next phase of the outdoor training.

In this arena, we discussed the different types of flora and fauna that could be safely eaten. In the animal department, we learned about the different nutrients supplied by the different parts of an animal. For example, the eyeball of a deer contains complex sugars, whereas the eyeball of a rabbit contains salt compounds. Although we didn't have a deer, we did have a live, domestic rabbit available for training. We were instructed on several ways in which to send bunny to meet its maker. One of them, wringing and snapping of the neck, was demonstrated by the instructor. I have hunted game since I was a pre-teen and have occasionally had to administer the coup de gras if the shot wasn't lethal. So nothing the instructor could do would have been bothersome to me. But it was to one of our group. On seeing the death sentence administered to the rabbit, our boy Teddy became visibly shaken. He paled and had to sit at the base of a tree for several minutes. So much for fearing Teddy and his munchkin-sized sword. I kind of felt sorry for him during the remainder of the Trek, as everyone relentlessly picked on him over the incident. This included warnings about the killer chipmunks and the dangers of being attacked by a chickadee. But back to the rabbit. This is where the training turned into a Dracula movie as far as I was concerned. The instructor, having dispatched the bunny, began to skin, clean, and butcher the little fella. In a survival situation, almost nothing of a freshly killed animal is discarded. There is nutritional value associated with nearly every part of the body. I was handed such a part by the instructor. And being a manly man, doing manly things with other manly men in a manly way, I popped the rabbit's intact eyeball into my mouth and swallowed it whole. I didn't even hesitate, because I didn't want to go through the same thing that Teddy had to endure. I pretended to chew it, but that wasn't ever going to happen. The reality was that it really wasn't so bad. It was like downing a Blue Point oyster or a horrendously large booger. I can't remember which.

As it was in fact November in Washington, the gear we were given was, indeed, winter issue. One of the more common items was the pair of eight-buckle galoshes. These were the same boots we wore as kids but very oversized and meant to be placed over a standard combat boot. One of the officers in my element put his on and decided to fasten only the lowest four buckles. This left the top of the boot wide open and flapping in the breeze. His every step caused the open tops of his galoshes to rub together, making a noise slightly less appealing than the "voot voot" backbeat of corduroy pants. Were he to attempt to escape and evade (E&E), he'd be caught the moment he sat up in his bunk. This fact was brought to everyone's attention when a deer wandered into our camp, and this young fellow produced his survival knife and rushed the animal with his galoshes flapping madly away. This "gentleman" could not figure out why the deer ran away. The young man obviously was neither Robert Goddard nor Werner von Braun.

That night, at supper, we decided to see what was provided to us. We had the rabbit, but that would have to be divided among five or six people. It was done with fishes, so why not a rabbit? We were also given one potato and one onion. This was to simulate our having stolen them from a local farmer or villager after bailing out. Next were our survival rations, which we'd find in our survival kits. "C" and "K" rations were a thing of the past, and meals ready to eat (MREs) were still ten to fifteen years into the future. The rations we were given were packed into what amounted to a Spam can: same size, same shape. Probably produced by the same manufacturer that provided containers to Hormel to encase their iconic meat creation. Inside, one would find a condiment package that included salt, pepper, sugar, instant coffee, and the ever-present P-38 can opener. The entrée would be a seriously dehydrated choice of cornflake bar, rice bar, or cornflake *and* rice bar. These things were about a half-inch thick and the same shape as the Spam can. They essentially consisted of one of the aforementioned cereal grains, honey, sugar, and a binder. They could be consumed in their present state, but that required real teeth and a jaw made of titanium. Those of us with any sense would break them up and stir the pieces into hot water from the campfire to make a sweetened sort of mush. Another goodie was the potato-and-cheese bar. Another dehydrated delight, this thing exploded into a dust cloud around the outside of your mouth when you bit into one, and the first mouthful would suck out every drop of moisture in your head. Knowing what we know today about the importance of water with regard to the digestive process, it's a wonder these things were allowed for human consumption, especially in a survival situation. The last item in the can was a chocolate bar. Once again, it was fashioned into the same size and shape of the previous items. It had the consistency of stone and didn't taste much better. It was like eating a piece of unsweetened Baker's chocolate that had been left in a mine during the California Gold Rush. The person who assigned the term "ration" or "edible" to these items was either quite mad or had a Machiavellian sense of humor.

We obviously needed to consume the rabbit first, so we doled out the pieces of rabbit, potato, and onion in the most equitable manner possible and began our individual suppers. Tommy, the other enlisted guy, and I decided to do a soup. Both of us were outdoorsmen, and knowing this, the officer types opted for the same thing. When it was time to eat, we noticed that the officers had finished their meals in very short order, while Tom and I appeared to keep eating from a bottomless mess kit cup. Being the only true campers in the group, Tom and I would drink the broth and keep adding more water to the solids. Once we got sated stomachs with all the broth, we ate the solids. I got a little tired of hearing, "Gee, I wish *we'd* thought of that," the rest of the night. As Tom and I belched the night away, the rest had to be satisfied with growling, unfilled bellies.

Our campsite was at the top of a steep hill. At the bottom of the hill was a small stream that was alleged to have trout in it. A couple of us climbed down and ran a hook line across the stream. We would see how well we did in the morning. Back at the top, we were tasked with constructing out sleeping quarters. We were provided with the same items we'd have available to us in a bailout survival situation. The most important piece of gear was the used parachute. Two adjoining panels are cut out and draped over branches that had been assembled in the following fashion: Two three- or four-foot sections were tied together at a ninety degree angle. Next, a seven- to eight-foot section was tied to the cross point of the first two, radiating away from the angle. The wide end of the parachute panels were draped over the larger end, while the narrow portion was fastened to the end of the longer pole. The finished structure resembled a pup tent without vertical sides or a back. A rain parka was stretched across the opening and became a door. The next step was hard. Six inches of pine boughs had to be layered across the ground inside the shelter to provide dead air space that would insulate the occupant from the frozen ground. It sounded simple enough, but we quickly learned that a plethora of happy campers had been through the school before us, and that explained why all the pine trees around looked so odd. Their bottoms were naked. The entire area was strewn with growth that resembled Christmas trees set atop poles. It took a bit of doing, but we were able to come up with suitable insulation.

A stub of a candle was provided in the survival kits, and several of us used the P-38 can openers to cut "barn doors" in the ration cans and placed the candle inside. It provided light for reading and, surprisingly enough, threw off enough heat to keep the shelter comfy. Having a mummy-style sleeping bag helped, too. Those things keep us very toasty.

In the morning, we woke up to temps in the teens. Nobody wanted to leave the warmth and coziness of their one-man shelter, but the instructors were having none of it. It's amazing how quickly one can dress when subjected to near cryogenic temperatures. Our first order of business was to climb down the hill and retrieve the brace of trout we caught. It was a wonderful thought, but Mother Nature had other plans. The creek had frozen solid in the night. So much for fresh trout for breakfast. We had to settle for cornflake and rice bar mush. Oh well, at least it was hot.

That day was filled with learning how to make snares and to cope when they turned up empty. I got an outstanding performance rating on the latter. But then, so did everyone else. The third day found us breaking camp and actually doing what the course name stated: we were going on a trek. More precisely, we were going to participate in terrestrial navigation. In other words, getting there from here, on the ground. We had topographical maps, and for some of us, they were very easy to use. Simply find a high point of land on the chart (that's nearby), locate that position on the ground, and begin walking toward it. Sounds easy, but the reality was that it could be very daunting. One aspect of the problem is that one is rarely on terrain that's absolutely flat. If the target piece of land goes out of sight due to walking through a depression or small valley, it can be very tough to regain that sight picture. Another issue is that it's not possible for a human being to walk in a straight line. The dominant leg will cause the person to circle in the direction of the other leg. In other words, a right-handed (right-legged) person exerts more power on the right leg step than the left. The result is that the walker will end up to the left of his intended target. But, the third issue is one no one would ever expect. This can be stated by the following: never allow an aircraft navigator to navigate on the ground!

Following the end of the navigation process—aka, becoming hopelessly lost—the instructors guided us close to the clearing where we were initially dropped off on the first day. The last portion of the trek was the technique of vectoring rescue aircraft to our position. In this exercise, we were handed a PRC-90 survival radio to talk to the rescue aircraft, in our case a Huey helicopter. We would listen for the sound of the aircraft and make a mental note of the direction of the sound while checking the heading on a lensatic compass. I won't go into any detail as to how this instrument is used, but it can save a lot of steps and perhaps a life. Using the compass, we had to give the pilot a heading and wait several seconds. If the noise becomes louder, he continues on that heading. Otherwise, we would have him turn in such a fashion as to get him pointed toward us again. The drill is complete when he's hovering over our head.

After the last student exercised his ability to make a chopper pilot throw up, the blue buses appeared and we began the long trip back to the base. One of the more pleasant aspects of going back was that we could go to the chow hall and pig out. Seems they always had "nicer" food in store for the survival school folks after a week of hell in the camp and then the boonies and we were ready to make pigs of ourselves. Standard air force chow hall food was generally bland at best but we were treated to steak with all the trimmings. There was a problem, however. Most of us suffered from an unexpected physical issue. With rations in such short supply during the training, our stomachs had shrunk. Although the food in the chow hall was of better quality, we simply didn't have any place to put it. All of us became full on what would have normally amounted to a midnight snack.

All in all, Fairchild was one of the most interesting schools that I'd ever attended. But it was about to be behind me (thank God), and I left with the feeling I could probably survive anything. That pipe dream went away on arrival at my next school.

CHAPTER 6

※

JUNGLE SURVIVAL SCHOOL

By the time I finished general survival, it was the second week in December. I'd spent my first Christmas in the air force in basic training in San Antonio, Texas. That was 1967. The next two Christmases were celebrated in Okinawa. I would have done better if I hailed from Florida, but being Pennsylvania Dutch, my Christmas roots included snow. This meteorological condition was rare in San Antonio and nonexistent on an island in the East China Sea. Displays of F-105 Thunderchiefs pulling Santa's sleigh only made the holiday time hokier and less traditional. So, I got to return home for Christmas before setting out for my next step in the pursuit of getting to Thailand by the longest method possible. Christmas wasn't bad, except that I got to drive my mother's 1964 Chevy II Nova from Ontario to Pennsylvania. That thing couldn't free fall out the back of a cargo airplane at seventy-plus miles an hour, which is what the ticket was written for by a New York state trooper, a mere ten minutes after crossing back into the United States. I had to follow him back up I-81 in the wrong direction, until we pulled into a very small town and parked at the local hardware store. There, the old gentleman behind the counter took off his nail apron, donned his judicial robe, and heard my case on the spot. I had visions of being forced onto a chain gang. This was a bit too surreal for me, so I said nothing, paid my $20, and got the hell out of there … at the speed limit.

After having spent a delightful Christmas with my family, I was driven to the International Airport in Philly to begin my journey west. The flight across the continental United States tended to be long and boring. But, the trip across the Pacific Ocean was yet to come, and I'd already done that once. I tried my best not to think about it.

I landed in San Francisco and made my way to Travis Air Force Base. Travis is one of the two major port call bases for all military types heading to Pacific assignments, East Asia and Southeast Asia. My destination was the Philippines and Clark Air Base.

Although some military aircraft have the ability to shuttle people from place to place, they don't have the capability to transport large groups of people on long distance flights. The military sends hundreds of people a day to overseas assignments and simply doesn't have the means to do so with its own fleet. The Pentagon, therefore, hires charter airlines to ferry its folks abroad. These charter companies use the standard civilian aircraft models but with their own paint scheme and amenities. Basically, these are older airplanes that have passenger seats mounted everywhere. If a particular model that is used by, say, United Airlines, can comfortably carry 102 people, the same model of charter aircraft could seat 130. The seats are not meant for human occupancy, and that can be attested to by any of the hundreds of thousands of sore-bottomed folks who have traveled in this fashion over the years. On a typical flight to an assignment over the Pacific, it could mean eighteen to twenty hours in one of those seats.

My arrival at Clark was uneventful (thank God). The one good outcome of such an uncomfortable flight was that, once on the ground, the passengers suffering from sore buns, cramps, jet lag, and any other number of maladies associated with overseas travel tend to be rather meek and robotic. They have "doe in the headlights" faces and are easily corralled and herded from place to place without as much as a whimper. We were shepherded to a Quonset hut–type building, got our paperwork done, and assigned to quarters. Looking across the nearby field, I saw that the "quarters" were wood-framed hooches with large, push-out, screened windows. Old-style tubular metal bunk beds were visible through the screening, and there was no sign of any form of air-conditioning. Not even a swamp cooler. A group of us began milling around and must have looked discouraged. We were approached by a Filipino lad, who apparently worked in the billeting office. He introduced himself as Pong and would be only too happy to set us up with nonavailability forms for a small gratuity. This wasn't exactly legal, but at this point, I didn't care very much about legalities or how much the gratuity would be. This meant sleeping in a hotel off base instead of Jed Clampet's mountain house. Actually, Jed's house would have been a bit nicer than the hooches.

As with all the courses that preceded this one, we started off in the classroom. We were given significant instruction on the flora and fauna found in tropical rain forests and jungles. They even supplied us with playing cards that had all of that information on them. If a plant was poisonous or otherwise harmful, the text accompanying its picture was printed in red. It's amazing how many plants there are that have toxic leaves but edible fruit and vice versa. Even the humble yet nutritious tomato is part of the nightshade family.

Another interesting aspect of the classroom portion was the "petting zoo", although you wouldn't want to actually pet anything in there. It was a zoological garden that was contained within a couple of hundred square feet of space in an open area near the classroom. The zoo contained all forms of plant life and cages containing everything from snakes to wild boars to giant rodents. The plant life was fascinating, as some of the vegetation in the warmer climates of the world have some very unusual properties. One plant, for instance, had broad green leaves that looked harmless enough. The underside of the leaves contains a chemical compound that causes a serious burn almost immediately upon contact. Yet another leafy plant has medicinal properties unlike anything one would attempt to imagine. Crushing the leaves releases a very potent blood coagulant.. Remember running down the street as a child and gripping a signpost to help turn a corner at a full run? During the course, one student apparently did that, utilizing a bamboo tree. Seasoned bamboo can be incredibly hard and will split open vertically. The edges of the split are razor sharp, and when this person did the signpost maneuver, he peeled back his entire palm. He obviously bled profusely, until one of the natives crushed several leaves and placed them in his hand. By the time the fellow got to the base hospital, the bleeding was completely stopped. The abovementioned native was not your stereotypical Filipino. These are the Negritos, who will be discussed momentarily.

The flora in the petting zoo was accompanied by fauna. Just about every rodent, nasty bug, predator, and reptile were on display. One of the more grisly looking critters was a wild boar. Although not a true predator, only the AC-130 is meaner if you piss one off. Gazing at a big, hairy pig with five-inch tusks makes you think twice about turning it into pork chops. The reptile display didn't disappoint, either. One always expects to see a cobra in a tropical environment, but there was one little poisonous rope that no one expected. This little fella was the banded krait. It's a rather small snake, averaging about a foot or so in length. But, it has one of the most toxic venoms known to nature. You might survive a cobra bite, but the bite of a krait is nearly 100 percent lethal without immediate medical attention. We jokingly referred to this snake as a "two-stepper," as that's about as many steps as you could take before succumbing to the venom.

Enter the Negritos. The majority of Filipinos are an ethnic mix of Polynesian or Asian people and the Spanish. Prior to the Spanish-American War, the Philippines had been a Spanish possession. The Negritos, however, are the aboriginal people of the Philippine archipelago. They are a rather diminutive, handsome people that, to this day, have scientists baffled about their origins.

Describing their appearance can be difficult due to the complexity of their physical makeup. They average about four feet in height but do not have the standard features of dwarfism. Their structural appearance is similar to

Caucasians, but their skin is the deep brown-to-black hues of sub-Saharan African descent. About the only thing that today's anthropologists agree on is that they didn't descend from African heritage. The Negritos can be categorized as hunter/gatherers. They use rice as their staple but enhance their meals with a huge variety of fruits, vegetables, birds, mammals, and fish. The instruments they employ to obtain all these goodies are as varied as the foods themselves. These will be discussed later.

On completion of the classroom phase of the course, we were to depart on the Philippine version of the Trek. The original Trek was about living off the land in the United States. The Philippine version, however, was as close as one can get to real survival without being shot down. No blue buses this time, either. We were loaded onto five-thousand-pound trucks and driven away from the base and into the jungle until the road ran out. The trucks dropped us off in a clearing, and we transferred onto HH-3 Jolly Green Giant helicopters, which took us an additional seventy miles. By the time we got to where we were going, any signs of civilization were only in our memories. In the clearing where the choppers landed, we were greeted by a host of Negritos. They were as curious about us as we were of them. As I looked them over, I noted any number of different weapons, including everything from homemade items to firearms. Each group of students, or element, had a Negrito instructor assigned to them. Ours was named Ernesto, and he liked to be addressed as Ernie. He was clad in a set of camo jungle fatigues and had an air of intense seriousness about him. I asked Ernie about the one little fellow carrying a shotgun. He had half a foot, so I jokingly asked Ernie if he'd accidentally blown off his foot with the shotgun. Ernie assured me that he did indeed lose his foot that way. Another native was clutching a bow-and-arrow combo that was twice his size. The bow alone had to be six feet long, and the arrow was nearly four feet in length.

I was curious about the arrow, as it didn't have a broad head point. Rather, it had projecting spines that resembled a frog gig. I asked Ernie if that's what it was, and he said no, it was for birds. I asked, "Does he shoot them out of the nest or perhaps on the ground?" Ernie replied that it was used to shoot birds on the fly. "Yeah, okay, right!" I suppose my doubt showed all over the place, because the little guy jabbered away, in his own tongue, with Ernie for a minute or two. Ernie then turned to me and said the fellow would be happy to show me an example for a few American cigarettes. Feeling fairly safe with such an insignificant bet, I agreed and let him have at it. He sent some of his pals into the tall grass, and they started beating the ground with whatever they were carrying and jabbering loudly in their native tongue. The guy with the bow knocked his arrow and kept it low. Now, I bow hunt. I, too, will knock my arrow until ready to fire. At that point, I'd raise the bow while simultaneously drawing back the arrow. I'll then take a bit of time to acquire my sight picture and select the correct range pin. By the time I released the arrow, about twenty to thirty seconds would have elapsed since first drawing back the arrow. And that's on a stationary target. Within a few minutes of bush beating, a bird about the size of a sparrow launched out of the grass at the speed of heat. Our archer raised his bow, pulled back the arrow, and released it at the end of the draw. The entire act took two seconds. The bird was promptly knocked out of the sky and pinned to the ground by the "frog gig." It seemed I wasn't the only one impressed. Just about every student who witnessed the Robin Hood anted up their cigarettes, and that Negrito was good to go on smokes for quite some time. It didn't take me long to realize that these little guys were the read deal, and I didn't need any more demonstrations. Some of the other items in their possession were spears, bolo knives, and widgets that defy description. The bolo knife is an interesting weapon. It is fashioned from the leaf springs of automobiles and more closely resembles a machete than a true knife. The Negritos were very well versed in their use, and I was just glad they were on our side.

The Negritos were also very good at navigating and hiding in the jungle, and this was the main factor that determined their participation in our training. The next demonstration proved that beyond a shadow of a doubt.

Our air force instructor had us face him, while Ernie left in the opposite direction to hide. We gave him a full five minutes head start. We were told that he was limited to a specific circumference around our camp and were given a specific time in which to find him. After ten minutes, we gave up. Ernie was probably on a neighboring island by now. Our instructor had us gather around him and called for Ernie to show himself. We all just about jumped out of our boots when Ernie stood up no more than ten feet away from his original position. He had used topography, grass, twigs, and whatever to conceal himself in plain sight. By this point, we began to understand the need and importance of this type of training.

The first day in the boonies was pretty much taken up by the transportation out there and by the demonstrations I've mentioned. The second day had us doing what I call the "nature walk." The students who were born and raised in the confines of a big city used other words to describe that part of our training. We had to find and identify most of the plants we'd been taught about and demonstrate their use. I found a wild lemon in a tree and felt as if I'd struck gold. One bite told me I was wrong. It was the most sour thing I'd ever tasted and caused my entire head to shrivel into my mouth. Fortunately, there were a lot of water vines around. These plants are virtually indescribable. They can be found as big as six inches in diameter or as small as two. The inside is not hollow, but the amount of absolutely pure water they contain make you think they are. In the American desert, you can squeeze a fair amount of potable water from a couple varieties of cactus, but it isn't really pure and turns toxic in a short time. The water vines, however, contain the equivalent of spring water. Cutting a foot-long piece of a six-inch diameter vine could fill a canteen to overflowing.

The final part of our time in the boonies was the E&E training. This made the Trek in Washington state look like an afternoon in the park. Once again, the Negritos were major players. Each of us was given a key ring with three dog tags attached to it. We referred to these tags as chits. Two of the chits were painted white, and the third was a bright red. I'll explain their meaning and use in a moment.

The object of the drill was to have us take off into the jungle, find a place to hide, and utilize all the skills and techniques we'd learned to that point. We would be given twenty minutes to get hidden and then a whistle would be blown. The whistle was the signal for the Negritos to begin the hunt. Their role was obviously that of the bad guys who were searching for us after we'd been shot down.

Although we're talking about a tropical jungle area, complete with mountains, valleys, nasty critters, and is located miles and miles away from civilization, this was still the Negritos house, and this fact would make itself quite clear as the drill went on. Here's the way the game was played. Once concealed, we had to do everything in our power to keep from being captured. Of course, this never happened. One was captured when the Negrito who finds us handed over a blue card. The card has directions as to what to do next. If okay, one hands the little feller one of the white chits. It's his incentive for finding you. At the end of the day, each white chit is worth five pounds of rice to the bearer. As mentioned earlier, a tropical jungle can be inhospitable, and a lot of unpleasant things can happen. If someone were injured or otherwise incapacitated, the Negrito would be given the red chit. He immediately takes it back to the lead instructor who, in turn, gathers a rescue team and follows the Negrito back to you. If one is okay after "surrendering," he would take a thirty-minute break and go hide again. Most of our students were never on a camping trip, much less turned loose in a mountainous portion of a Philippine jungle. Nearly everyone was captured within about ten minutes. I was a bit luckier than most, having grown up hiking, hunting, and camping. I found myself a spot with the most natural protection available, thereby avoiding ripping up the jungle trying to camouflage myself. To a Negrito, a couple bent or missing branches has the same impact on him as we would have arriving home and finding pry marks around your door lock. My hiding place was on the side of a fairly steep hill. The steep hill provided cover to my right. Behind me were fairly thick brush and overgrowth that couldn't be penetrated with a chain saw and a weed eater. To my left, the downhill side was also full of dense growth that was virtually impossible to see through, much less traverse. Besides, it wasn't very likely that someone would attempt to crawl up that steep hill just to be stopped by a wall of thicket and tangled vines. The area in front of me was the least protected. It's actually how I was able to slide into my little refuge, which resembled a vegetation cave, so I figured that's where I needed the most help. I lay prone, facing the opening. I used leaves and branch material I grabbed from an area about two hundred yards from where I hid so as not to give myself away. I positioned this debris in such a way as to look as natural as possible but figured that would be the direction from which I'd be seen and captured.

For what seemed like an eternity, I was visited by every kind of critter that one could imagine on a South Sea island jungle. Crawling by me or over me were rats, snakes, spiders, and every type of insect known to man, and a few that weren't. When it finally came, it was a total surprise. I felt a tapping sensation on my downhill arm. I looked over to see a small, black, disembodied arm and a hand waving a blue card and tapping me with it. I never saw a person, just parts of a person. I surrendered a white chit to the arm and got the hell outta there. I found my way to the break area and discovered another survivor there. We talked and shared our stories of how, where, and what we did over the past hour or two. Both of us were hidden for about forty-five minutes, which was actually pretty good. (Felt like forty-five hours to me.) By that time, I wasn't really in the mood to go hide again and tried to figure out what I could do to avoid it. Just then, a Negrito appeared in the clearing. He was bouncing along, silently, looking for his next victim. I stopped him, handed him my second white dog tag, and wished him a nice day. I wasn't very politically correct in those days. As I handed him the tag, I said, "Here ya go shorty. Go get some rice." What the hell; they didn't speak English, and that's probably the only reason I'm still here with all my body parts intact to relate the story.

The trip back to Clark was simply the reverse of the trip to the boonies. Jolly Greens to the end of the road and then trucks back to the base.

Once again, I had to admit the air force had come up with some very valuable training. All the stops had been pulled, and anyone headed for aerial combat in Southeast Asia would be as prepared as humanly possible.

Next stop: the Southeast Asia theater of operations and the Vietnam war.

CHAPTER 7

★

ARRIVING IN SOUTHEAST ASIA

The flight from Clark Air Base was uneventful. Our first stop en route to Thailand was to Ton Son Nuht, South Vietnam. Ton Son Nuht was the name of Saigon's international airport. The folks who were being stationed in Vietnam disembarked here. The rest of us were curious why we weren't allowed to get off the airplane for even a minute. It was probably due to some political rationale or perhaps to keep the clerk typists from claiming combat status by setting foot in a combat zone.

From Saigon, we flew to Don Muang, Bangkok's international airport. Don Muang was also the main base for the Royal Thai Air Force (RTAF). Looking across the field from the civilian terminal, one could see just about every version of aircraft produced by the United States since the early fifties and a few from before that. At the time, the RTAF flew several aircraft types, but the majority were T-28s, A-37s, and F-5s.

After deplaning, the people who would be stationed near Bangkok and the southern provinces went to one part of the terminal to await ground transportation to their final destinations. The remainder of us were loaded onto a C-141 that headed for the up-country bases. We arrived at Ubon RTAFB and began the processing drill. We did our thing with the personnel folks and were issued mailboxes, meal cards, and billeting. The latter was a bonus, as the enlisted flyers had initially been billeted in hooches, which, like in the Philippines, were simple, wooden structures that may have had a ceiling fan. By the time I got there, the flight engineers, IOs, and gunners were being housed in a large two-story cinder block building complete with air-conditioning. As time went on, I was to find that this little perk was but one of the reasons we flying enlisted were loathed by all the other enlisted types on the base. I'll get into the other rationale a bit later.

During our walk about the base during in-processing, I bumped into Joel, the fellow I was stationed with in California when we both volunteered for the gunship program. We agreed to meet up at the end of the day. Joel had arrived at Ubon a few weeks ahead of me, and I learned that he was living off base in a bungalow. Actually, quite a few of the GIs lived on the local economy. It was a lot less stressful than living on base, even with air-conditioning. Part of the reasoning also had to do with socializing. There were a plethora of bars and bathhouses off base, and the cost of these places was about one-tenth of their US counterparts. There was also the *tiloks* (pronounced tea-lock). This was a Thai word that essentially meant girlfriend or sweetheart. These were gals, about our age, who lived in the bungalow and performed every service from clothes washing, cleaning, cooking, to, as the Japanese put it, "pillowing." Surprisingly, this arrangement was not terribly expensive. A bungalow could be rented for about $30 a month, and the food, bought locally, was very inexpensive. A few bucks for spending money, and the occasional bauble or clothing item, kept the "lady" happy. In all candor, living off base was a relief, considering the job we had to do for Uncle Sam. Living in a cubicle with four or five other guys could get a bit claustrophobic after a while. Besides the bars, and so on, the local town also had movie theaters that showed current films. For us *farangs* (pronounced fah-longs), there was a small room in which you could hear the actual soundtrack. For the locals sitting in the auditorium, they were treated to a Thai overdub. I often thought things got lost in translation, though. For example, in a scene where the guy gets the girl and love is in the air, one could hear the people in the auditorium laughing. I suspect that the Thai dubbers used a bit too much artistic freedom in the translation.

If we needed to remember our roots, the base also had a movie theater, base exchange, Airman's Club, NCO Club, Officer's Club, barbershop, and one or more Thai-run eateries that provided fairly decent American and local cuisine. And, I shouldn't forget AFRTS, the military run local radio station. Each base had one and was *Good Morning, Vietnam*-esque.

CHAPTER 8

✪

THE FIRST MISSION

When we first arrived at the 16th Special Operations Squadron (SOS), there were no "hard" crews. The Ops (operations) folks would simply grab one person of each specialty, and that would be the crew for one mission. I must state, however, that the gun crews *were* hard crew and always flew together. Since we worked on weapons in a blackout environment, we couldn't afford to mix techniques and personalities. Therefore, the five-man gun crew was always together. It must be noted here that several months after arriving at Ubon, the squadron finally did go to hard crews, which ultimately made for a better mission.

My first combat mission was my first mission at Ubon *period*. There was no time or inclination to perform training missions in-theater for the new kids. That's what Lockbourne was for. So, on that night of January 15, 1971, I was told to find an out-of-the-way place to sit and watch what was going on. This was otherwise known as a "combat orientation flight." As the night progressed, I found it to be a great technique. It's one thing to fly around Lake Erie and Ohio at night, but it's a whole other animal when you're flying over a neighborhood in which the residents want you to die. The airplane used on the night of my first combat mission was 630, known as *Azreal,* the Angel of Death. This fact will come into play for me, as will two others, long after I'd retired from the air force in 1989.

The initial portion of the mission was unremarkable. The only major difference from what I saw in Ohio was that, shortly after takeoff, we performed the sensor alignment. Immediately after takeoff, we climbed to our working altitude and set up an orbit over the base. On top of a small shack at the east end of the runway was a small transmitter. It sent a directional signal that was picked up by one of the electronic components in the aircraft. That signal was displayed on the sensor operator's gear, and it allowed us to fly a perfect pylon turn around the shack. Once that was achieved, each sensor operator slaved his sensor to the position of the beacon. Adjustments were made that allowed every sensor to "look" at exactly the same point on the ground. It makes sure everyone is looking at the same spot. But this operation becomes especially important in the event we are tasked with a TIC or troops in contact. In this instance, one misaligned sensor could send several high-explosive rounds into a friendly's position, causing a very bad day for everyone concerned.

Once the sensor alignment was completed, we took up an easterly heading toward the Laotian border. We kept the lights on while over Thailand and were only required to wear a standard headset. Once we crossed the border, or "fence," into Laos, we turned off all the exterior lights and placed the interior lights to red. We also donned our helmets, which were not true flight helmets. They were ballistics helmets and weighed a ton. The good part of it was that this variety of helmet would stop shrapnel from cracking your coconut. There was one exception to the exterior lights being switched off, and that was the canned beacon. This was the standard red, rotating beacon on the top of the fuselage, near the vertical fin. It was also known as the anti-collision light. The boys in the sheet metal shop fabricated a funnel shaped shield that was placed over the beacon, skinny end down. This prevented the beacon from being seen from below or the side of the aircraft but would allow the fighter escorts to see it from their higher orbiting position or "perch." If we ever needed our escorts to attack something on the ground, it was vital for them to know our position before attempting to dive toward to ground and through our altitude. Once we were twenty-five miles over the fence, all the interior lights were extinguished, except for the peanut lamps with red filters that shown on the feeders of the 40 mm and 20 mm guns. Attempting to place a four-round, twenty-five-pound clip of ammo at exactly the correct angle, in the dark, was nearly impossible. Each gunner had a NiCad flashlight that had two bulbs and lenses. The bulb in the clear lens was removed, and a rubber plug was placed over the bulb in the red lens. The plug prevented white light from escaping from the exact front of the light, which was unprotected. The most common use for these lights was for making repairs to a jammed or otherwise broken gun. We held the rectangular-shaped flashlights in our teeth to enable us to use both hands for repair work. After a month or two, one could always tell who was a Spectre gunner by the teeth marks at the base of his flashlight.

As per my pre-takeoff instructions, I found a place to sit and watch. I selected an area on the left side of the aircraft, between the 20 mm flak curtain and the NOD operator. The flak curtain was a heavy, dense, two-inch thick fabric wall that surrounded the 20 mm guns. Being a multi-barreled canon, these guns spun at nearly five hundred rpms as they fired. If a round went off prematurely or the gun came apart and disintegrated, the curtain was the only thing between you and the next world. The NOD was an infrared night scope that was mounted in the crew entrance door. The space I chose was about three feet across, so I had plenty of room to observe the 20 mm gunner and the right scanner. I wasn't able to see what was happening with the 40 mm guns, as they were in the rear of the airplane, and I wasn't about to get up and walk around the dark airplane trying to sneak a peek. I knew that all of that would come in time, so I sat with my back against the fuselage and kept track of the goings-on.

We ultimately found some trucks on the Ho Chi Minh Trail and began the attack. So far, nothing much was happening that was different from training, except that I had to keep remembering where I was. It certainly wasn't Ohio, Auntie Em. We successfully took out the few trucks we found and leveled off, looking for some more. One thing that should be explained at this point is that although we weren't given specific targets, like a bomber would be given, we were assigned a numbered area in which we were to patrol. These areas were about the size of one or two counties in the States. I learned early that areas 7 and 14 were exceptionally dangerous. I don't recall to which area we were assigned the night of my first mission, but it could have been either of those.

After searching for another half hour, the BC operator informed the crew that he had a "mover." To recap, the BC, or Black Crow, was a system that could detect vehicles from the emissions given off by their ignition systems. It was very similar to the static you'd hear in your car while listening to the AM radio and driving under high tension lines. A "mover" was the term given to a moving vehicle on the trail. Since the BC had the ability to detect these emissions from up to twenty miles away, it was nearly always the first sensor to find the bad guy's trucks. And because it had directional ability, the BC data would be transferred to the onboard fire control computer. This, in turn, was fed to an instrument on the other sensor operator's panels, and a needle on an indicator would direct us to the approximate position of the vehicle. Once there, either the NOD (later the TV sensor) or the IR sensor would slave to the BC, and we'd have an electronically enhanced visual on the target. That data was fed into the computer, and the pilot would turn to his gun sight, which was mounted in his left window, and symbols displayed in the sight allowed up to take up and orbit directly around the target. As mentioned earlier, one of the symbols in the sight represented the position of the gun and was fixed. The other symbol moved and represented where the sensor was looking. The pilot simply maneuvered the aircraft in order to superimpose the symbols. When that occurred, he pressed the trigger located on his yoke, and the gun would fire. The computer did the math, and when the symbols were superimposed, wind, airspeed, altitude, air density, and several other parameters had already been taken into consideration. If the system was working, a three- or four-shot burst from the 40 mm or a three-second burst from the 20 mm usually meant a destroyed or severely disabled truck.

So, we followed the BC to the target area, and one of the visual sensors found the targets. After about two orbits, we opened fire. Seated where I was, I was able to look out the crew entrance door. Most of the night, I only saw blackness. The next time I looked out, I saw what looked like Roman candles, rising at our eleven o'clock position. They were beautiful, crimson red balls. I kept thinking, *Those are real pretty. I wonder what they are?* This is when the mind goes into denial and mortality is threatened. It took me a full thirty seconds to realize that they were 37 mm antiaircraft rounds, filled with two pounds of high explosives, and someone I didn't even know was trying to kill me! At the forty-second point, I was about to climb onto the flight deck and tell the pilot to take me back to Ubon. He could come back afterward if he wanted to play war. At fifty-five seconds, I came back to reality and realized that this is what I volunteered for. Besides, all these other guys didn't seem to mind, so I wouldn't either. Funny thing is that in a few more weeks, we would take it as a personal insult if we didn't get shot at. Ah, the crazy things that bounce through our empty heads when we're young (and not terribly smart).

Note: To this day, the sight of a red star shooting out of a Roman candle at a fireworks display evokes some sort of response from me. In the first few years after my time in gunships, the response was nearly always not pleasant.

CHAPTER 9

✪

THE ESCORTS

No C-130 variant is known for speed or agility. That was reserved for the world of fighters and fighter/bombers. The 130 was built to carry fairly heavy cargo into and out of hot areas from small, unprepared, or even grass runways. The AC-130 was hobbled even more simply by its mission. The standard C-130 can fly up to twenty-three thousand feet and has a cruising speed of slightly over three hundred miles per hour. In the gunship version, while on target, we flew at an altitude of less than ten thousand feet when firing the 40 mms, and lower still for the smaller caliber weapons. And all of this at an airspeed of 160 knots, with 40 percent flaps. We were, in essence, a big, black, very slow target that flew around in circles for five hours. That should give the reader a better appreciation as to why we were so adamant about any light leaking from the airplane. Even the smokers on the cargo deck were required to cup their hands around their cigarette when lighting up. Another problem was the "gunner's moon." This occurred when there was a full moon and was also generally exacerbated by a thin cloud deck above us. It had the same effect as making bunny shadows on the wall. The airplane stood out like a sore thumb.

Having said all of that, it's obvious that we were somewhat exposed and not readily able to defend ourselves. In our offensive role, you would go away if you were the bad guy and we were after you. In a defensive role, we were sitting ducks. Enter the 497th Tactical Fighter Squadron, better known as the Night Owls. The boys of the 497th flew F-4s, as did many other units in Southeast Asia. But the Night Owls were a bit different. Their aircraft had their bellies painted black, and they were nearly always our escorts. They obviously had other roles to perform, but when flying with us, we felt invincible. No other fighter unit was as well versed in our mission and tactics. Additionally, they had the most varied assortment of ordnance that I'd ever seen on a fighter. No two hard points contained the same munition. They had everything from dumb bombs to laser-guided bombs to cluster bombs. And they were always equipped with infrared or radar-guided air-to-air missiles for their own defense. While we were doing our thing at a very low altitude, they would orbit at an altitude about double ours, waiting for the call from us that might not ever come. But, when we *did* call, we were glad to have them around. One of the more usual uses for our little friends was when we encountered an antiaircraft gun that was partially hidden by foliage or was otherwise difficult for us to deal with. We would use a technique known as "sparkling." We would pull the HE ammo out of the 40 mm and load tracer rounds. We knew approximately where the AAA was and would fire at or around it. The fighter pilot would see the tracer, follow it down, and puke high explosives all over it. This technique was 100 percent effective, and we never had the same gun come up on us twice after it was visited by our escort. One factor needs to be mentioned at this point. Prior to diving onto the sparkled target, the fighter pilot would call out, "Bullseye," over the radio. That was meant to let us know that he was about to enter our orbit, and we were to stop firing. In the world of good things and bad things, hitting an F-4 with our gunfire would be a really bad thing! Surprisingly enough, this almost happened. The following is the story as it was told to me:

As in a sporting event, one can't tell the players without a program. So, this section is added to describe Lieutenant Colonel Ken "Grouchy Bear" Harris and one mission that was out of the ordinary. Grouchy Bear, or GB as we affectionately called him, was the 16th SOS squadron commander during my time at Ubon. Ten minutes with him, and one had an undeniable sense of how he acquired his nickname. A totally businesslike, "mostly" by the book, individual whose gaze could stop global warming. And, it could get a lot worse if he was in a bad mood. Atheistic aircraft commanders who had done a naughty something and had been summoned into his presence could be seen genuflecting prior to entering his office. The local joke was that his face would crack if he ever smiled.

The story goes that he was getting his hours in and did so as the AC on this particular night. (He occasionally flew the right seat as well, just for shits and giggles and hours.) Squadron commanders didn't fly as often as the crews, due to their administrative duties, so they got their hours whenever they could. On this particular night, they were over their assigned target area when they were joined by the escorts. As mentioned earlier, we normally flew with the Night Owls. However, we occasionally had to fly a few missions with escorts from other units and other bases in Southeast Asia. On this particular night, the escorts were F-4Es out of a base in Vietnam. To be fair, I won't mention their base or their callsign. They were very good at their assigned missions but terrible at escort duties. They didn't know our tactics and rarely knew the meanings of our coded radio transmissions. We used to joke that they were lucky to hit the ground with a bomb. I recall that we even used to put them on targets like forks in the road or puddles of water just so they'd first go Winchester (run out of ordnance) and then go away. I think we'd have rather flown against a radar-guided AAA site than to have them tagging along and getting in the way. So, GB is out over the trails, and the F-4Es are escorting. There came a point where the gunship either needed a flak suppression run or to have a target struck with CBU. GB contacted the fighters and began sparkling for them with the 40 mms. He eventually became concerned when, after about a dozen rounds were fired, nothing was heard from the fighter. GB continued firing, until the fighter came up on radio and started a filth-filled diatribe about tracer ammo going over his canopy and almost being hit by it. His initial mistake was showing up in the first place. His second was getting on the radio and cussing out the gunship and making an ass out of himself. He complained mightily about how the gunship endangered his multimillion-dollar fighter and putting his crew at risk. By the time GB got back to Ubon, he had sparks coming out of his ears and fire coming out of his eyes. After debriefing, he went to his office and dialed up the wing commander at the fighter's home base. Legend has it that if you were an aircraft that had become lost anywhere in Southeast Asia, you could simply look at the ground and locate a glowing red phone line. Just follow it east to Da Nang or west to Ubon. Bottom line: this "anal cavity" never declared, "Bullseye" and just dove into the middle of the gunship's orbit. The story never did mention what became of that fighter jockey, but it's a sure bet that he had an interesting chat with his wing and squadron commanders the next day. I would love to have been a fly on the wall for that one.

Like every negative story ever told, there is always a positive one to counteract it. In this case, the positive side is a gentleman everyone called The Animal. He was a captain and flew with the Night Owls. He got his nickname honestly. In sports, you never wanted to be on the opposing side. This was especially true in games that featured a ball. In handball, racquetball, and tennis, you were quite likely to eat the ball when it was returned at the speed of heat. The same was true with volleyball. No one ever spoke of the mark the ball left if The Animal spiked it. They spoke of the crater that was created. As a fighter jockey, he was no less "enthusiastic." This fact was borne out on one particular mission in which The Animal was one of the two escorts that flew with us. At some point in the mission, we had a 37 mm gun that was becoming too accurate on each of our orbits. We couldn't find it and called on the escorts for some assistance. The Animal had used up all his ordnance on previous targets, but his wingman still had a couple of cluster and gravity bombs. As mentioned before, external lighting was a no-no, even for the fighters. Another one of our code words was "Christmas Tree." This describes a situation in which all the external lights were on. Another bit of trivia is that the F-4 was equipped with breather doors in the wheel wells. These doors would open when the gear were down and allow extra air to be pulled into the engine. Due to the shape and location of these doors, the F-4 would howl like a banshee at low power settings with the breather doors open. It's possibly the reason the airplane was named the Phantom II. Obviously, lots of lights, lots of additional noise, and a very low airspeed during night combat were not a good mix if survival was your main concern. However, without knowing the precise location of the gun, this is precisely what The Animal did. He went Christmas Tree: gear down with landing lights on, and breather doors open at an engine idle setting. Needless to say, an airplane capable of fourteen hundred miles per hour, noisily falling out of the sky at slightly over one hundred fifty miles an hour made for a pretty tempting target if you were manning an antiaircraft gun. The 37 mm opened up, and The Animal jinked his way through all the tracers headed his way. At about one thousand feet above the ground, The Animal pulled up the gear, turned out all the lights, and went into four stages of afterburner while aggressively climbing for altitude. Although the lights were out, two afterburners look like twin high-powered propane torches in the night and still made for a pretty lucrative target. The 37 swung around and kept firing. What the AAA gunner (and we) didn't know was that The Animal's wingman was right behind him, blackout. Following the tracer paths back to the ground and identifying the muzzle flash of the gun, its position was given away. We heard, "Pickle, pickle, pickle," over the radio and watched through the gun ports. ("Pickle" is the code word for releasing ordnance.) A few seconds later, the CBU he had released opened and sprayed a doughnut-shaped area about one hundred feet across with bomblets. The two five-hundred-pound gravity bombs made an impression on us as well. It was a sight to behold, especially when the ammunition stores began exploding. It was as if a fireworks factory had exploded. I often wondered what The Animal's backseater thought about all this. After all, wherever The Animal went, the backseater went as well, with no choice in the matter. I found out later that the backseater was as loyal as a fine hound and would have followed The Animal through the gates of hell. On that night, it seemed to me that he did precisely that.

CHAPTER 10

✪

COLONEL SAM

As stated in an earlier chapter, we initially didn't fly as hard crews. This mind-set eventually changed, and by spring of 1971, we were indeed assigned with the same folks and became hard crews at last. My crew's aircraft commander (AC) was Lieutenant Colonel Sam Schism. Sam was a tall, forty-something, partly balding gentleman from Tennessee. Looking at him, Colonel Sam reminded me of the farmer with the pitchfork in the painting *American Gothic*. He spoke with a soft voice that included a very pleasant Tennessee drawl. He was the type of individual one came to like and admire in a very short time. As a pilot and aircraft commander, we always felt quite safe when flying with him. He never showed any signs of stress, no matter what type of trouble the airplane might have been in. This particular trait will be addressed again in another part of the story.

During the early months of 1971, after our hard crew had been established, we were feeling a bit jinxed. We weren't able to chalk up more than one or two trucks a night, whereas our contemporaries were getting eight or more. On one particular mission, I was working the #3 40 mm and called the pilot on interphone. I bet him a steak dinner that we couldn't get ten trucks that night. He took the bet, and I was feeling pretty good at the thought of a lieutenant colonel buying a lowly buck sergeant a steak dinner. On that mission, we didn't get ten trucks … we got twenty-five, and it turned into a DFC mission for the entire crew. Being a man of my word, I met Colonel Sam at a hotel in downtown Ubon several days later. Of course, he had to order chateaubriand. But then, this was Thailand, and I doubt the entire meal cost me more than $10.

Colonel Sam also gained hero status in the minds of our crew on March 25, 1971 when we suffered a direct hit by a round of 37 mm antiaircraft. That story will be explained in detail in the next chapter.

An interesting bit of trivia is that Colonel Sam's real first name is William and middle initial is O. To this day, I have no idea where he picked up the name Sam.

Colonel Schism is also remembered for the work he did with Robert Reinlie on behalf of a large group of fellow warriors. Beginning in 2001, they filed suit to preserve health benefits promised to WWII and Korean War veterans by recruiters of that period.

Sadly, Colonel Sam passed away a few years ago. He will be missed by his crew and by anyone with whom he had contact. On a side note, I live in a fairly small town in Upstate New York. There is a county airport here that sees only light aircraft and doesn't even have a small regional airline to service the area. On the same day that I found out that Colonel Sam had died, a C-130 did a touch-and-go from the airport before flying directly over my house at about five hundred feet. Military airplanes never fly into or out of our dinky little airplane patch. I'm not a superstitious person, but I've often wondered if there was a greeting, a farewell, or other cryptic message associated with the incident.

First Lady Photos

First C-130 flight by tail #53-3129, The First Lady. Note original "Roman Nose" before introduction of standard radome.

The First Lady in a repair nose dock the day after the hit.

Photo of damaged area behind nose gear. 37 mm shell entered just forward of the debris seen just aft the wheel-well bulkhead.

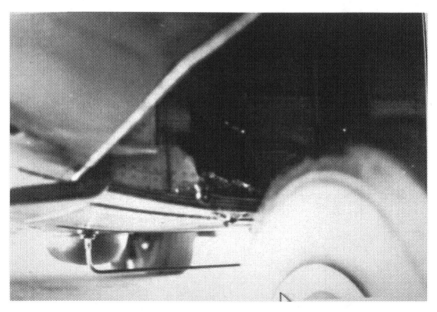

B&W shot of bulkhead damage. The round detonated just on the other side of that jagged hole. Photo courtesy of Ed Wakeman.

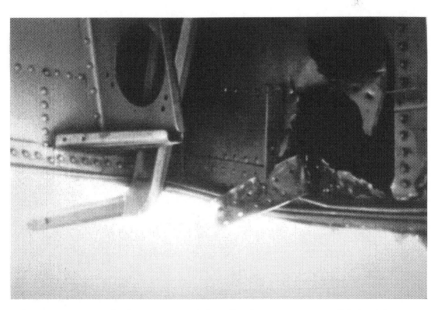

Close up B&W of wheel-well bulkhead. Photo courtesy of Ed Wakeman.

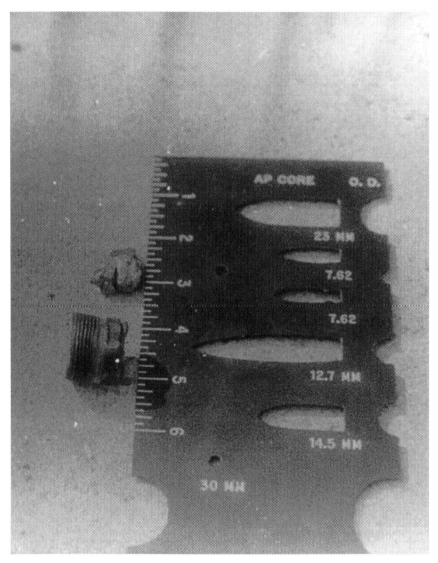

Two pieces of shrapnel recovered from The First Lady and gauge that investigators use to determine calibers. Photo courtesy of Ed Wakeman.

Jeff in the Right Scanner's seat.

Jeff in combat gear before a mission.

Jeff in his party suit – AFTER the party.

General Survival School photos

Clearing in the forest on the Trek at survival school.
Photo courtesy of Dale Compton.

Shelter made from parachute panels during the Trek.
Photo courtesy of Dale Compton.

A VERY young Dale Compton at the General Survival Trek
in WashingtonState. Photo courtesy of Dale Compton.

Jungle Survival School Photos

Typical open-bay hooch provided for students.
Photo courtesy of Dale Compton.

Entrance to the Jungle Survival School classroom and "petting zoo."
Photo courtesy of Dale Compton.

HH-3 Jolly Green helicopter used to transport students to the boonies in the Philippines. Photo courtesy of Dale Compton.

Hut in a clearing. At 70 miles away from the base, this constituted "downtown." Photo courtesy of Dale Compton.

Aircraft General Photos

Tail # 623, The Exterminator, at Lockbourne AFB. This aircraft was used for training and was Jeff's first-ever gunship flight.

Tail #623 nose art.

An AC-119K Stinger used for training at Lockbourne AFB.
Photo courtesy of Dale Compton.

NOD Operator peering through NOD in training at Lockbourne.
Note standard white aircrew helmet. Once in-country, we used
ballistics helmets in combat that were painted olive drab.

Two gunners relaxing near 40 mm guns before take off. Note open sensor operator booth door and the 55 gal. drums used to catch 40 mm brass casings after firing. The aisle gunner is also visible in the background. Photo courtesy of Ed Wakeman.

Walking back to the aircraft after a maintenance delay. The person in the center with the six shooter on his right hip is our resident cowboy, Dale Compton.

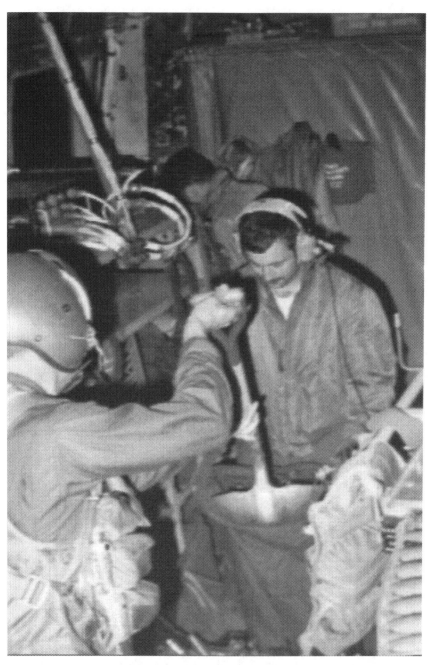

Shoveling 20 mm brass into duffel bags. Gunner holding bag is
Cliff Pound. Gunner at Right Scanner window is possibly Jeff. The
person holding shovel is either Dale Compton or Ed Wakeman.
Ed is pretty sure it's himself. Photo courtesy of Ed Wakeman.

Before: Crew arrival at tail # 014. Note three-bladed props in 1971.

After: Same aircraft, tail 014, at Griffiss AFB, NY circa
1988 after four-blade prop and paint upgrade.

Airborne Photography

Looking out the ramp door just after leaving the
runway at Ubon, enroute to a mission.

Photo of F-4 parking ramp during takeoff.
Photo taken through Right Scanner's window.

Photo of an AC-130 launch as seen from the ground.

Ubon's gunship parking ramp as seen from
the air, immediately after take off.

At our working altitude over the base performing sensor alignment before heading out to the Trails. The funnel-shaped objects at the end of the barrels are flash suppressors.

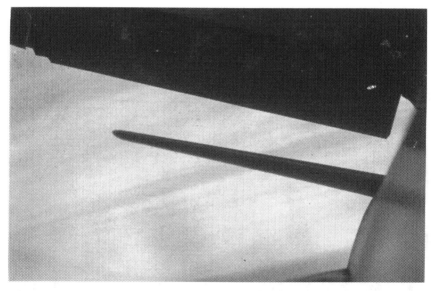

View looking aft along the fuselage from Right Scanner's window. Another gunner, not knowing what I was doing, nearly pushed me all the way while grabbing for me thinking I was FALLING out. I breathed funny for a few minutes after that.

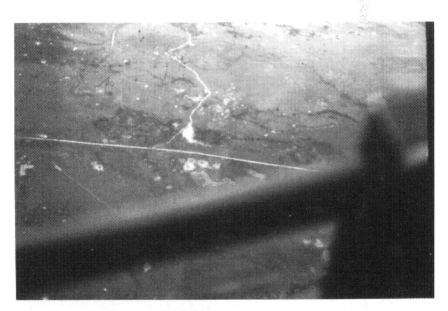

A rare daylight mission. The white smoke is from a rocket fired by a FAC. He suspected 200+ bad guys in the two sets of trees on either side of the road. 10 minutes later, there weren't ANY. Note bomb craters everywhere.

Crew Photos

HQ building for the 16th SOS. Wording in shadows:
"Fabulous Four-Engine Fighters of the Wolfpack".

Our Aircraft Commander, LtCol Sam Schism. Note the gun firing trigger on the yoke in front of his thumb. Behind his head is the Heads Up Display in the left window.

Ed Panarese, our crew's Navigator.
Photo courtesy of Dale Compton.

IR operator Larry Michalove, left and BC Operator Ed
Wakeman, right. Photo courtesy of Dale Compton.

Our Sensor crew before the advent of the TV and
FCO. Larry and Ed in front; Hank Sullivan in back
row was our NOD, and later, LLTV Operator

Cliff Pound, one of our five gunners, demonstrates a clip of 40 mm HE being loaded into the Bofor's feeder. Cliff was one of the original Sam's Hams. Photo courtesy of Dale Compton.

Cliff in full combat gear with chest pack parachute attached. Photo courtesy of Dale Compton.

Dale looking out Right Scanner's window on
headset, prior to crossing the Fence.

Dale in full gear at the Right Scanner's position. To give you an
idea as to why most of us have hearing problems today, that black
wall with the vertical stripe outside the window is the engine
cowl of the #3 engine. Photo courtesy of Dale Compton.

The Weapons

The 40 mm Bofor's canon with 55 gal. brass drums.

Exterior view of 40 mms.

The two 20 mm Vulcan canons with Cliff holding back the flak curtain for the shot. Photo courtesy of Dale Compton.

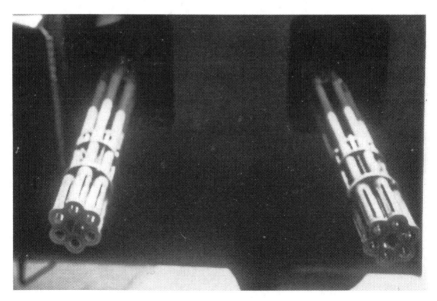

Exterior view of 20 mms.

Prometheus

Scanned photo of the damage suffered by tail #044,
Prometheus, from the Ubon base newspaper in Nov 1971.

Actual photo of damage to Prometheus's engines taken through
RT Scanner's window. Photo courtesy of Ed Wakeman.

Jeff's party suit.

Name tag, wings, and American flag on left
sleeve mandatory on all party suits.

The standard right breast emblem. Also mandatory on all party suits.

Another "humor" patch in reference to the first air kill by the 8th TFW.

Lots of folks had this patch in tribute to how
the enemy used to refer to us.

Sam's Ham's crew patch for Spectre Crew 7.
Photo courtesy of Dale Compton

Jeff's Battle Damage Qualified patch from the direct hit on the First Lady.

The wet-down after the end of Col Sam's champagne flight.
Note the empty 40 mm ammo cans on the edge of the ramp.

Ron Bienias –CP
Larry Michalove – IR
Hank Sullivan – NOD/TV
Sam Schism – AC
Photo courtesy of Ed Wakeman

Democracy Monument in Bangkok.Celebrates Thailand's
conversion to a constitutional monarchy in the 1930's.

One of Bangkok's numerous museums.

Raised traffic-cop platform at a busy Bangkok intersection.

One of the less-busy busy streets in Bangkok.

Guards at the King's palace.

Tourists cruising one of Bangkok's many canals.

Floating diner on the canal surrounding the Bangkok Zoo.

Life as a child along the canal.

Old and new on the canal.

Flattened grilled bananas at the Bangkok Sunday market.

The Big Buddha. This large statue is located about an hour from Ubon.

Dale at one of the two-thousand-year-old Buddhist stone statues
near the Big Buddha. Photo courtesy of Dale Compton.

Black market offerings in a small shop at the
Thai–Laos border near the Mekong River.

Aerial view of downtown Ubon (left) showing bridge over
Mun (pronounced *moon*) River to the village of Warin.

Money tree. As with other parts of the world, the Thais
hold parades to raise money for religious causes.

The neighborhood kids around my bungalow.

Food vendor in Ubon's open market.

Children at the open market.

Food vendors along the road to Ubon. These are found at
every small town or village throughout the countryside.

Houses on stilts near the MunRiver shoreline.
During the monsoon season, this area is underwater.

Fire fighting at Ubon. We saw the smoke from this fire on our way back from a mission. Rumor had it that the fire was a result of a sapper attack.

View from the top floor of the Ubon hotel looking toward a newer Buddhist temple, or Wat.

Philippine band member on samlar (Pedi cab) with driver in passenger seat. You could get to anywhere in the city for five to fifteen cents.

CHAPTER 11

✪

THE FIRST LADY

The date was March 24, 1971. The night started off as usual, with the crew briefing and sanitization of our flight suits. The sanitization of a flight suit meant that we were not allowed to wear patches of any kind that might belie our unit or base of operations. I still recall hearing the pilot brief, "AF ID, dog tags, and green money." Those were the only items we were allowed to carry with us. The "green money" was for the possibility of having to land at another base for some reason.

This is the story about the journey into history of the most famous C-130 ever built by Lockheed Aircraft.

After the end of the Second World War, the air force recognized the need for a large, heavy-lift cargo airplane. Since the 1930s, the C-47 Dakota was the military's standard cargo aircraft. It was rugged and dependable. So much so that of the thousands manufactured, several hundred were sold to several foreign governments. But with piston engines and a mere six-thousand-pound payload capacity, the C-47 was simply not big enough to handle the increasingly larger loads required by an increasingly larger US military. The C-47 was augmented by the C-46 and C-119 Flying Boxcar, but they, too, suffered from the same inadequacies. The C-54,

C-123, and C-124 cargo planes were a step up from the C-47. But some of the same problems arose once again. The C-123 was a two-piston engine model, while the C-54 and C-124 were not suited for short and soft field takeoffs and landings. So, in 1951, the air force put out a request for an aircraft that would meet or exceed all of its requirements. Lockheed (now Lockheed Martin) won the contract, and by 1954, the first production C-130 Hercules had rolled off the assembly line and was ready for its first flight. The serial number, or tail number, of this first C-130A was 53-3129. We would later refer to our tail numbers by the last three digits.

Moving forward in time to the 1960s, 129 found itself being modified and pressed into service as part of the original cadre of AC-130 gunships. The following is a description of one of its more memorable combat missions:

I've made it a point not to name names in this story, as I've forgotten several, and there's always the problem of offending someone when describing something they did or didn't do. This will be the rare exception. Crew 7 consisted of our AC, Lieutenant Colonel Sam Schism; CP, First Lieutenant Ron Biennas; Table Nav, Major Ed Panarese; FE, Technical Sergeant Floyd England; NOD operator, Major Hank Sullivan; IR, Major Larry Michalove; BC, Major Ed Wakeman; and IO, Staff Sergeant John Roye . The gun crew (we called ourselves Sam's Hams) consisted of the following, with their position identified for this particular mission. I was in the right scanner's seat, Dale Compton on the 20s, Cal Brown in the aisle, and Cliff Pound on the 40s. Sadly, I do not recall who the fifth gunner was. After preflight and engine start, we taxied toward the runway. We hadn't taxied very far, before I noticed a great deal of liquid coming out of the bottom of one of the right-side engines and reported it to Floyd. He came down and took a look. It turned out to be the purge and dump (P&D) valve, which was stuck open and pouring JP-4 all over the taxiway. The maintenance folks came out and told us there was nothing they could do about it in a short time, so we taxied back and parked on the hardstand. We unloaded our gear and took the bus back to the squadron. It began to look as if we were going to be cancelled when we got the call telling us that they found us another airplane. So, back onto the bus and out to the flight line. The tail number of the replacement aircraft was 129. Back then, most of us were in our early twenties and didn't know anything about the significance or history of that particular tail number or the nickname, *First Lady*. All gunship gunners were laterally trained bomb loaders and weapons weenies before training in gunships. For example, Dale loaded flare and chaff cartridges on RF-4s, while I loaded hard bombs and nukes on B-52s. None of us had ever heard the name *First Lady*, and even if we had, it wouldn't have had much impact on us, because 129's original nickname may have been *The Arbitrator*.

We obviously had a very late takeoff, and by the time we crossed the fence, it was the early morning hours of March 25. After patrolling our assigned area for a very short time, we came up on what is commonly referred to as a target-rich environment. The good news was that we had movers all over the place. The bad news was that there were three or four 37mm guns all over the place as well. I had never seen so many guns in such a small area before, so it definitely got our attention. Initially, the AAA wasn't very accurate, and we spent most of our time counting the number of rounds that Gomer fired at us, so we could report the numbers to the intel folks in Saigon. There was a point in the orbit where the moon was at about the two o'clock position, and a gun located just outside the path of the orbit would open up. I would lean way out the window 'til my eyes watered and could see the muzzle flash of the gun when they fired. It looked like someone taking flash pictures just a couple of seconds before the tracer ignited. This gun, too, wasn't much of a threat, and I would call out the number of rounds over interphone. This went on for about a half dozen or so orbits. It got so predictable that I'd start leaning out the window as soon as I saw the moon appear off the nose. By the time the moon was just off the right wing, they'd open up again. A few orbits later, I was leaning way out again when several rounds of 37mm came from inside the orbit, which is an area the right scanner can't see. One round just missed the spinner on the #4 prop, while another just missed the wing tip. I sucked myself back through the window so fast, I must have looked like a turtle that had just gotten spooked. I began putting pressure on the mic button to report twenty-five rounds, accurate, when I heard the noise of what seemed like a large rubber mallet striking a piece of hardwood on a metal table. Initially, it sounded like someone had dropped a clip of 40 mm in the back. But this is where "denial" comes in. First off, I'm in an open window, with a very loud turboprop engine running about fifteen feet away. Second, I have my back to the booth, essentially a small, enclosed room that is effectively blocking the front end of the cargo compartment from the aft. There's obviously no way I could have heard anything from the aft gun area. We rolled out and began running the emergency procedure checklist. The first order of business was interphone check in. Each crew position would report in and relate his status. Everyone reported in except the NOD operator. Dale went to check on him and found where his interphone cord had been cut by the shrapnel. He was okay, and Dale informed the crew. We immediately contacted Moon Beam (nighttime airborne command and control center; ABCCC), declared an emergency, and headed west to Thailand. After we'd all settled down and determined that the airplane was still flyable, we began checking out systems. At the pilot's request, I put my NiCad light between my teeth and turned around in the scanner's seat to monitor the RH side hydraulic accumulator. More than anything else, it resembled forty-cup coffee percolator. There was a gauge glass on the side of the accumulator that showed the amount of hydraulic fluid in the container. During normal gear lowering, the red fluid would drop about an inch within the glass tube and then rise again. When he put down the gear handle that night, the red fluid disappeared all the way down the tube and sprayed out somewhere else in the airplane. This required us to put the main gear down manually, which isn't fun. It takes three hundred sixty turns with a speed handle connected to a crank system that hadn't been used since the airplane was built in the 1950s. We all took turns at it, and it had to be done separately for each main gear. It occasionally took about thirty seconds to make one full turn on the speed handle. A dozen turns would wear you out. The copilot has the responsibility to lower the nose gear manually, using a totally different procedure. He does this by lifting up an access plate on the floor near his right foot, turning the exposed valve, and using a pump handle located on the floor to the right of the valve. It was just about then that Floyd, who had previously come down from the flight deck to inspect everything, came up on interphone and briefed us on the damage. We'd been hit in the belly, just aft the nose gear wheel well bulkhead. There's a raised wheel-well pocket that that can be seen on the cargo deck floor, directly under the flight deck. It has approximately a six-inch by six-inch Plexiglas window that allows one to inspect the nose gear from inside the aircraft. Floyd reported that the Plexiglas window had been replaced by a rather large, jagged, hole that measured in excess of a foot square. The dimensions of a C-130's nose-gear wheel well make it cavernous. The strut and wheels only take up about 50 percent of the space. The remainder is chock-full of hydraulics and electronics. Because of the damage there, we weren't able to tell the condition or position of the landing gear, as the indicators on the pilot's panel no longer functioned. After the CP did his manual pumping routine, Floyd looked back into the inspection hole with a flashlight and pronounced the nose gear down. Meanwhile, Cal and I opened the case of hydraulic fluid that was stored under the electronics rack in front of the scanner's seat and began refilling the accumulator that had emptied itself during the gear-lowering attempt. We obviously weren't going to attempt anything with the standard gear system again, but those accumulators serviced more systems than just the landing gear. At one point, we had a lull in our activity, and I climbed up onto the flight deck to see what was happening in pilot-land. What I saw had a very calming effect on me and left an indelible impression about someone who would soon become a hero in my eyes. Colonel Sam was flying with one hand on the yoke and one foot resting on the forward portion of the throttle quadrant. Colonel Sam never exaggerated anything, nor did he take things for granted. Seeing his demeanor let me know that we were safe, in good hands, and that we'd make it home okay.

We had just crossed the fence back into Thailand, when Floyd unexpectedly appeared on the cargo floor once again and disappeared back under the flight deck with his flashlight. He later said that while still up on the flight deck, the hair stood up on his neck, and he felt that something was terribly wrong. Well, thank God for Floyd's neck hair! The nose gear had cycled itself back up, and with no working indicators, we had no way of knowing it. So, take your choice: divine intervention or neck hair. He had the CP do his hand pump thing once again, but this time, Floyd remembered something from his tech school days. He grabbed a stick of some kind and reached into the gear well with it. He told us later that there's a little white mark on the strut that can only be seen when the gear is locked. He used the stick to overcenter some kind link and locked the gear down manually. Okay, so everything is peachy dandy. The gear is down and locked, the flaps worked, all of the engines are running, no more leaks were detected, equipment is stowed, and we're all strapped in on final. My crash position was on the floor with my back to the booth. We touched down, and I knew all was good in the world once again. Yeah, foolish me. Colonel Sam called out, "Hang on, crew … we got no brakes!" I pictured myself surviving through all that crap while airborne, just to be killed in a ground loop at the end of the runway. He reversed the engines (louder than I'd ever heard before), and we decelerated in pretty short order. When we were about five miles an hour, Sam told everyone to unstrap and get ready to, "Get the hell away from this airplane!" Just as I had unstrapped and begun to stand, the CP decided to try his brakes, and they worked. If anyone ever wondered what a redundant system was, there's your answer. The airplane jolted to a stop, and I went flying, ass over teakettle, across the plywood 20 mm brass box that was built into the floor (insert unkind officer/pilot epithet here). We all exited off the ramp to be nearly run over by every vehicle on base with a rotating red light on its roof that had chased us down the runway. Ed Wakeman recalls the ominous number 13 on the crash truck (apparently way too many "nasty" thirteens in Ed's career). We ran and stood off in the grass, several hundred feet away, and waited for the all clear to approach the airplane. Out of the darkness, this character in civilian attire approached us and asked who the pilot was. We all pointed to Colonel Sam. Note: Every base had a technical representative from the companies that manufactured the airplanes assigned there. This guy was the Lockheed tech rep for Ubon, who wanted to know how we got the airplane back. In his familiar Tennessee drawl, Colonel Sam replied, "Just flew it … Piece of cake." During this conversation, we "youngsters," with the immortality complex, were joking about cheating death and, "just another day in Spectre." That's when the tech rep replied to Sam, "This airplane shouldn't have been flyable with that amount of damage in those places." After that statement, I begin to understand the end of a Billy Joel, "Piano Man" lyric that goes, "as the smile ran away from his face." At that moment, the smiles ran away from all our faces. When the aircraft was deemed to be safe to walk around again, I went up to see the damage. Had I seen that hole while we were still airborne, surely goodness and mercy would have followed me, because I'd have grabbed my chest pack and gotten the hell out of that airplane!

In the following days, a subsequent inspection showed the full extent of the damage. The Nav and NOD operator were found to be two of the luckiest puppies alive. The 37 mm exploded directly under the Nav's seat and directly behind the NOD position. The floor at the Nav's position had a horseshoe-shaped pattern of holes around the seat but had left the seat itself untouched. The NOD had a similarly shaped pattern of holes around the circumference of the crew entrance door, where his sensor was located. Additionally, the life support techs found shrapnel fragments in his parachute backpack. He was leaning over into the scope when the round exploded. Had he been sitting upright, there'd be another name added to the Vietnam Wall.

John Roye was one of the best IOs with whom I ever flew. I found it inconceivable that he never saw the Triple A that hit us, nor called for an evasive maneuver. I approached him the next day and asked him about it. As it turns out, there were so many accurate rounds heading our way, that any maneuver would have caused multiple hits rather than the single one that found its mark. He said that in the little amount of time he had to make a decision, he figured he was better off keeping that knowledge to himself rather than put the aircraft in greater jeopardy.

So, let it be known that at approximately 1:45 a.m. on March 25, 1971, the *First Lady* was gang raped by shrapnel and otherwise horrifically violated.

But she maintained her dignity and, beaten and bloodied, safely brought her crew home. Therefore, if any of you get the opportunity, go to Eglin AFB, Florida, and visit her in the Air Force Armaments Museum, treat her with respect and honor. She deserves it, and she's earned it.

Over the course of the past year, I was able to locate Ed Wakeman, our BC operator. We've shared e-mails, and I finally remembered to ask a question that had been on my mind since 1971. Why his preoccupation with the number 13? Originally, I figured him to be a superstitious type. But, his answer sent chills down my spine. On the night we were hit, we had thirteen crew members onboard, our callsign was Spectre 13, our patrol sector was area 13, and the first crash truck to meet us on the runway was #13.

As with *Azreal*, the *First Lady* is another AC-130 that will prove to be an important addition to my life after the air force.

CHAPTER 12

✪

TCHEPONE

The antiaircraft encountered over the Ho Chi Minh Trail was very fluid in its location and intensity. Nearly all the guns were on wheeled carriages and were highly mobile. They often followed the larger convoys in order to provide protection on a 24/7 basis. On any given night, we may have encountered two or three guns near a moderately traveled portion of the trail. If we went to the same area on the second night, the guns may be gone. We understood that and lived with it. There were, however, a few areas in Southeast Asia in which the AAA was numerous and permanent. The two most notorious places were known to everyone with even a slight knowledge of the Vietnam conflict. These were the North Vietnamese city of Hanoi and the port city of Haiphong. These were two of the most heavily defended areas in the world during that time. But, there was one other place that was nearly as lethal as the Hanoi and Haiphong areas but was unknown to those who generally flew over Vietnam. It was the Laotian hamlet of Tchepone. The mere mention of that name would make the hair on our necks bristle. Even the fast movers, like the F-4s, didn't like to go there. Tchepone was to the Ho Chi Minh Trail what Kansas City is to the railroad industry and was located just a few miles into Laos, just south and east of the demilitarized zone (DMZ) in Vietnam. Just about every road on the trail traversed Tchepone. It was the locus for nearly all of the truck traffic. Additionally, there was a river that went through the town, and it had branches into nearby waterways and canals. There were always minor truck parks along the trail, but Tchepone looked like the parking lot at the Mack truck assembly plant. That being the case, Tchepone sported a total of over twenty antiaircraft guns of every caliber. The heaviest gun we were aware off at Tchepone was the 85 mm. This monster could shoot you down from more than thirty-four thousand feet. Needless to say, we avoided Tchepone like the plague.

One piece of navigational equipment that was found on the AC-130 was LORAN, which is an acronym for long-range navigation. Before the days of inertial navigation or GPS, this old-fashioned piece of electronic gear was about the only way we had of knowing, with some precision, approximately where we were at any given time. The theory of operation is triangulation of low-frequency radio waves. Just tune in three stations, and you're good to go. The one drawback to this system is that it's very vulnerable to weather. And when the monsoon season hit Southeast Asia, the entire LORAN system could be seriously compromised. We were to find that out one night.

We took off in questionable weather during the rainy season and prepared for a dull and boring night. The weather was so bad around Ubon that we wondered if we'd even be able to take off. I recall the Nav telling the pilot that he saw a "sucker hole" on his radar, just off the end of the runway. Since the majority of the Trail was dirt roads and paths, truck traffic was virtually nonexistent. Our mission description was night armed reconnaissance and interdiction. During the monsoon season, we referred to it as night armed cloud recce (short for reconnaissance). The first part of the mission ultimately revealed a bit of humor. Since the Ho Chi Minh Trail was washed out, there was no reason for any AAA to protect the convoys. This made for a miserable, boring night. When you're being shot at, the adrenaline flows, and the warrior mentality comes out. In other words, you keep warm. But at this time of year, flying in the thick, wet air was like walking through a London fog during winter. There were a lot of openings in this unpressurized aircraft, and when we flew through the low-level clouds, the cloud would actually come inside the airplane and soak you like a reverse steam bath. It was a wet, soaking cold that penetrated right down to the bone. On this night, I was working the 20 mms and was sitting with my back to the sensor booth. Every now and again, someone would call "Here Gomer, Gomer, Gomer," over the interphone. I assumed it was one of the sensor operators, looking for a truck. This went on for the better part of an hour, and eventually, I had to relieve myself. I unplugged from that interphone and headed to the back of the aircraft, where the urinal was located. Once there, I plugged in the interphone located there and began to take care of my business. Once again, I heard the, "Here Gomer, Gomer, Gomer," call over the interphone, but this time it sounded different. There was a whooshing noise associated with it, and I began to think it was the IO, hanging off the ramp. I walked up to the edge of the ramp to find the IO had a five-cell flashlight, waving it madly toward the ground and yelling, "Here Gomer, Gomer, Gomer!"

In about another hour, the humorous aspects of the mission took a decidedly different turn. The area in which we were working was close to the Vietnam border and very near the DMZ. We were approaching the four-and-a-half-hour mark and knew the return to base (RTB) call would be made within the next few minutes. At this point, the nav came up on interphone and informed the pilot that the LORAN had just died, most likely due to the weather. The pilot asked for a heading, and the nav reasoned that since we were just about due east of Ubon, we should turn due west and hold that heading until he could use his navigational skills to find precisely where we were. Within about four minutes of taking up a westerly heading, just about every sensor operator called out over the interphone, claiming to have multiple movers. Because the NOD had since been replaced by the low light level TV by this time, the pilot asked for the TV to be the primary input into the computer and immediately took up an orbit. Trucks were everywhere, and the TV operator selected one to begin the attack. We had fired three rounds of 40 mm when the entire sky lit up with tracer. We had to initiate some incredibly violent evasive maneuvers and found it very hard to get back into an orbit. We were guessing that nearly one hundred rounds of 37 mm and 57 mm had been fired at us in the course of about thirty seconds. The 57 mm was easy to identify, because, when watching its tracer, the rounds would quickly overtake and pass the strings of 37 mm that were usually fired first. In this instance, we had a twin 57 mms come up on us, and that can cause a variety of biological responses when it's aimed at you. Suddenly, the nav comes up on interphone again and tells the pilot, "Put the flaps up, firewall the throttles, and get the hell outta here!" Our pilots were very good at never asking questions, and ours did as he was told. Just about the time we began firing, the nav had figured out where we were. After we were safely out of danger, the pilot calls back and asks the nav, "What the hell was that all about?" The nav replied, "That, gentlemen, was Tchepone." The reaction of the entire crew was the same. Had a proctologist been giving any of us a "finger wave" at the time, his finger would have been snapped clean.

In 1972, we lost three AC-130s to ground fire. Two of those losses occurred in the airspace directly above or adjacent to Tchepone. In total, thirty-plus friends were lost during that horrible year.

Looking at Tchepone today via Google Earth, it's hard to picture this little village as one of the most dangerous places on the face of the earth. It gives the impression of a tranquil country place, where one might like to retire. If you would like to see this place on Google Earth, type in Xepon, the Laotian spelling of the town. The original town has since been "moved". The original can be seen 2.1 miles to the southeast, astride the river where two roads intersect from Hwy 9 to the north. It still looks like a truck park.

CHAPTER 13

✪

THE GENERAL

The mission day started out pretty much as usual except that it was my turn to go out and preflight the guns. On mission day, one of the five gunners was tasked to go to the flight line and perform checks on all the guns and the ammo loads. In those days, the 40 mm ammo was stored in cans that were placed on the opposite side of the fuselage from the guns and were strapped to the floor. The majority of the 20 mm ammo was loaded into each gun's ammo can and ready for use. Each can contained fifteen rounds of ammo. We had additional 20 mm stored in smaller cans that were strapped to the floor in the aisle. This ammo would be strung together and loaded into the guns can in the event that it was needed, which was a rare occurrence. With no lighting, this was another arena in which a gunner definitely earned his pay. Another part of the gunner's preflight was to ensure that the guns were set up correctly with regard to the azimuth and elevation settings. Each gun had a sight-in card that described the elevation and azimuth positions for a specific altitude, and the pre-flighting gunner needed to crosscheck these settings. This got me back to the squadron a tad late for the mission briefing. As I was walking toward the door to the briefing room, I was met in the hallway by this old guy in a sterilized flight suit, asking where the briefing was for Spectre 21. I showed him where it was, and we went in. Although rare, we occasionally had someone fly with us for an orientation flight, and given his age, I figured it was a Lockheed or LTV tech guy. LTV was just one of myriad vendors associated with the AC-130 program, and their folks occasionally flew with us to check new equipment installation and use. We also had crew members of other combat aircraft who would come along for a joy ride on the world's best airborne six-shooter. But again, his age seemed to make that type of scenario dubious. During the briefing and preflight, I never gave the old guy much thought. When we got to the flight line, I didn't see him and suspected that they already had him up on the flight crew deck during our interior preflight and preparation for takeoff, as that was the norm in order to keep visitors out of the way. We performed the normal engine start, taxi, and takeoff, and headed out to the trails. After we began attacking the first set of trucks, I see this guy heading toward the back of the airplane. I was working the #4 40mm at the time, which had me facing forward. The one thing that was very dangerous about the 40 mm Bofors cannon was the ramming shoe, which recoiled about six inches out the back of the gun. We were always very careful to keep our hands away from there during firing, as it could take off a hand and never slow down. There was also the issue of an expended brass round heading out of the back of the gun at worp seven as the gun was firing. Well, the old guy comes back to the gun to take a closer look. He bends over and sticks his face to within an inch of the rear opening of the gun. The gun is firing, so I put the clip of ammo in my left hand and reached out my right to prevent him from getting any closer and to warn him of the danger. Between the clip of ammo in my left hand and the gun firing, I became somewhat unbalanced, and my right hand pushed him backward rather than stop him. Also, he was leaning over the fifty-five-gallon brass drum, which meant he wasn't in a stable position. Between that and my push, he went backward, tripped over an open 40 mm can, and fell unceremoniously to the floor, landing quite harshly on his butt. Whoever was passing ammo helped him up (gun still firing), but he went forward and back to the flight deck. It was an hour or two later when the pilot announced that we were diverting to NKP (Nahkon Phenom), another base in up-country Thailand. The next thing out of his mouth was for the gunners to watch out for the "General," as he was leaving the flight deck and coming aft. I looked at the other gunner and asked, "We got a general on board?" He shrugged and said he didn't know. Well, at twenty-three years of age, 1+1 never equaled 2 for me, so I started making myself look presentable so, I could meet the general (whoever he was) and get some points. I looked forward and saw a figure climbing down the ladder and stopping to talk with the front gunner. Then he proceeded to the rear, and as he got closer, I noticed it was the same little old man that I had put on his ass. He glared at me like Methuselah, and I thought I was gonna turn to stone. He kept on going to the ramp, got a load of IO talk, and headed back to the flight deck. I just knew my career was over and that I'd be in Leavenworth for assaulting a general. The hour or so that it took us to fly to NKP was the longest, most miserable hour of my life. After we taxied to base ops at NKP, he came aft again to get off the airplane. As he approached, I "hid" behind my headset and pretended I was doing something to the gun. Then, a hand goes up to my shoulder and turns me around. It's the general. He puts out his hand and starts pumping mine with an enormous grin, saying, "That was the most fantastic [yada yada yada] thing I ever saw!" My mouth dropped to the floor. I composed myself and tried to apologize for pushing him. He said something like, "That's okay, son. I was pretty pissed at first and told the pilot what had happened. He said I shouldn't have been so close to an operating weapon in the first place and that I was lucky you didn't toss my ass out the ramp." Talk about a sigh of relief! We later found out that he was a three-star, vice commander, PACAF, and was on an inspection tour of some kind. His presence in-country was classified as a standard precaution, because they didn't want the North to know a high-ranking officer was flying over the trails. Too tempting a target, I guess. At any rate, one of the things I learned that night was that dodging a bullet doesn't always mean evading a stream of 37 mm. Given my behavior, I often wonder how I managed an entire AF career and still retired as a senior NCO.

CHAPTER 14

✪

SPECTRE'S URBAN LEGENDS

This portion of the story is intended to relate some of the better tales I've heard but never personally witnessed. As with current urban legends, and rumors in general, most every tale is based on a modicum of fact. I will attempt to relate some of these stories without the usual embellishment that is found in so many GI tales.

The Cambodian Reservoir—Nothing noteworthy here with regard to the players. Rather, the mission itself is the key player but needs a bit of clarification. We rarely flew during daylight hours. The exceptions would be those rare instances in which Intel and/or on-scene folks guaranteed the absence of any AAA emplacements or, as in this instance, the target area was in Cambodia, which basically had no antiaircraft capability. This is a semi-humorous retelling of one such mission.

On this particular mission, the AC-130 was assigned to interdict some enemy water traffic in a reservoir. If I remember correctly, the reservoir was man-made and had flooded a valley that had a hill in the middle. On that hill was a Wat (Buddhist temple or pagoda). When the flooding of the valley was complete, the hilltop became an island within the reservoir, with the pagoda as the only remaining structure left intact and above water.

Moored all around this island were several hundred sampans, rafts, barges, and small boats, all belonging to the Khmer Rouge or Viet Cong and all loaded with ammo, explosives, and other types of war material or other contraband. As per our rules of engagement (ROE), most structures, and especially religious buildings, were *always* off limits, and any legitimate target had to be over twenty-five meters away from any other type of structure. Since the flotilla was moored virtually at the temple doorstep, the gunship couldn't fire. The crew relayed that fact to ABCCC and was told to loiter as long as fuel was available. The crew called them about hour later and was given essentially the same instructions, with the caveat that something would be done to aid in our predicament. Sometime later, the right scanner reported numerous small, silver-gray airplanes off in the distance but couldn't tell their heading. If someone had told me that small, "silver" airplanes were nearby, especially during daylight hours, my flight suit would have been full of every sort of waste material my body was capable of producing! Most of North Vietnam's fighters were that color, and a jet fighter against a slow-moving gunship was absolutely no contest. The pilot told the scanner to keep an eye on them and report if they got closer. Within five minutes, the scanner reported that the smaller aircraft were heading toward the gunship but still couldn't identify them. Another call to ABCCC, and the crew was told not to worry about it. What a timely call; all fifteen flight suits must have been fairly soiled by this time. In a few minutes, the crew could make out the bogeys. They were Cambodian, propeller-driven T-28s, and they started peeling off and diving toward the water, like John Wayne in a WWII movie. They went in with small bombs, rockets, and strafing. What the hell? It was their country, their temple, and certainly not restricted by US doctrine. After the initial attack by the T-28s, the boats and so on began fleeing in all directions, and the gunship opened up and ultimately went Winchester in pretty short order. The one major bit of Intel gleaned by the crew was that most of these rafts were made out of bamboo, and a bullet had to be put through each segment to get it to sink. This was one of those missions about which an old flyer's adage must have been born. It states, "Combat flying is described as hour upon hour of sheer boredom, interspersed with moments of stark terror."

Dave B.—Dave was one of the most colorful characters of the early Spectre era. He was part of the original cadre of crew members for the AC-130 program and was already a pseudo-celebrity by the time I arrived at Ubon in 1971. The stories of him and his sidekick, Oley, were numerous and exciting. I will relate a couple that I know are somewhat factual. I found Dave via e-mail and asked him to confirm or deny some of the tales. With the exception of one of my favorite stories, which Dave told me was untrue, the remainder of the tales had their basis in factual occurrences.

One of the things that was taboo was to bad-mouth Spectre, and a lot of that happened at Ubon. It wasn't unexpected, as the bad-mouthing came from the other enlisted folks stationed there. The problem stemmed from the fact that we, too, were enlisted but were drawing separate rations (paid to eat outside the chow hall), earned flight and combat pay, and were tax-exempt due to our combat status. As a buck sergeant, I was taking home as much as a technical sergeant, which was two grades higher. Needless to say, this caused a great deal of animosity with our non-flying contemporaries. Inevitably, someone in the Airman's or NCO Club would shout, "Spectre Sucks," and a fight would ensue. But, this behavior also followed us off base. Dave and Oley frequented a couple of local bars called the Fairlane and the Jaguar Club. Dave and Oley remodeled both places more than once when someone shouted something "unkind" about Spectre.

Dave had a rubber frog that he took on combat missions for good luck. Oley kept threatening to steal the frog and cut off its legs. During a party in the Spectre's officers' hooch, Oley did what he promised. Several crews had mascots and were reluctant to fly without them. When Dave's crew learned what happened to Freddie the Frog, they were a bit nervous flying without him. Before continuing, it should be explained that each combat flying unit in Southeast Asia has a sister squadron at another base. In the case of the 16th SOS, our sister unit was the Jolly Green Giant search and rescue folks stationed at Nakon Phenom. These guys were just about as maniacal as we were, given that their job was to hover over a downed crewman as he was being hoisted out of the jungle, all the while being shot at. It seemed reasonable that all the nut cases should be grouped together in sister squadrons. Well, somehow, the Jolly Green guys heard about what happened to Freddie and showed up at Ubon with a new one, which they presented to Dave at the NCO Club.

Although Dave had gone back to the States by the time I arrived, he found his way back to Ubon in 1972 or 1973. We had lost three airplanes and most of their crews in 1972. This was a black time for Spectre, and feelings—not to mention morale—were pretty low. Most of the non-flying enlisted types were smart enough to keep their rude comments to themselves during this period. However, one night a couple of gunners stopped by the base Thai restaurant to get a bite to eat on their way to go fly. At the back of the restaurant, at a point farthest away from the door, a group of enlisted folks were seated and obviously had too much to drink. Seeing the Spectre types, they felt compelled to comment on how Spectre finally paid the piper with the loss of three aircraft and crew the previous year. The tone of this comment had a, "Serves you right," component to it. As these guys were about to go fly, they weren't in any position to react. But, on arrival at the squadron building, they got on the phone and called the NCO Club and asked to speak with anyone from the 16th SOS. The person who answered the phone was Dave B. Dave collected about a dozen Spectre types and walked the rather short distance to the Thai restaurant. On arrival, they noticed that the drunken group was still there and proceeded to walk toward them. One of the brave but drunk diners decided to stand and say something stupid to the approaching Dave and his entourage. One of the other drunks grabbed his arm and convinced him to sit down rather abruptly. Dave began the rather one-sided conversation by asking them to repeat what was said and if they thought the death of American servicemen was funny. Another of the men seated with the group stood and, in tears, tried to explain away the situation. Not being impressed by the explanation, Dave took another step forward and said something to the effect of, "You denigrate and insult the memories of your fellow countrymen, who gave their lives in combat. Now, we're going to clean your clocks!" The reaction of the drunken diners was reminiscent of the Keystone Cops. One even jumped through a closed window in an attempt to escape Dave's wrath. To this day, I don't have any idea as to the outcome of this incident.

Another favorite story about Dave B. had to do with marksmanship. Part of the survival equipment issued to us was the S&W Combat Masterpiece, in .38 Special caliber. We were given about twenty rounds of ammunition for it, and six of them were tracer rounds. This was basically to augment the flares and gyro jets that we would use in a rescue situation. Dave and his crew were on a mission and taking a great deal of AAA. Normally, we wouldn't load our pistols until we were in a survival situation. For some reason, Dave had his .38 loaded with the tracer ammo. At one point, the AAA was too accurate and a left break was called. Dave was riding the right scanner's seat that night. Becoming annoyed at the accurate 37 mm, he pulled out his .38 and began firing at the 37 mm tracer heading toward the aircraft. On one of the shots, the flight engineer confirmed that Dave's tracer intersected a round of AAA, and it detonated off the wing. At the altitude they were flying, the rounds of 37 mm that missed striking the airplane would self-destruct about another thousand feet higher. That being the case, there wasn't any other reason why the 37 detonated early, so Dave was given credit for shooting down a round of AAA with a pistol.

Dave is still alive and has moved back to Ubon to retire. He returns to the States from time to time for the Spectre reunions.

Unfortunately, Oley died under mysterious circumstances in Africa while flying as a civilian crew member in some type of cargo aircraft.

The Floating IO—As mentioned in the crew descriptions, the IO had what can accurately be called the most hazardous on the airplane. Hanging halfway out of the aircraft, tethered by a one-eighth-inch steel cable is not *my* idea of a good time. The evasive maneuvers he called for were always violent and occasionally caused minor injuries to the gunners in the cargo compartment. During a particularly violent maneuver, the airplane broke right (positive Gs), climbed (more positive Gs), and dove (negative Gs). Anyone seeing films about NASA's Vomit Comet can see what happens when positive Gs are followed abruptly by negative Gs. The end result is weightlessness, and things begin floating off the floor. The 40 mm gunners were instructed to drop their clip of ammo and make love to the feeder of the gun when that happened. On performing this technique, one finds one's feet above his head. That is precisely what happened during this maneuver. Most everyone came down pretty hard after the last break was completed, and the pilot asked if everyone was okay. Everyone answered that they were, indeed, okay, except the IO. He didn't respond at all. The pilot called him again, and this is how the conversation went.

Pilot: "IO, Pilot."
IO: "Go ahead, sir."
Pilot: What's your status? Are you okay?"
IO: "Request permission to board the aircraft."
Pilot: "Say again?"
IO: "Request permission to board the aircraft."

The pilot then called back to the gunners to find out what was wrong with the IO and what he was talking about. Looking up to the ramp, the gunner could not see the familiar heart-shaped silhouette of the IO's butt in the dark. The gunner cautiously approached the ramp and found the static line going over the edge of the ramp. He followed it with his fingers and peered over the edge. The IO was outside the airplane, dangling in the slipstream that actually became buoyant at the portion of the aircraft that abruptly swoops upward near the tail. The IO looked as if he were in one of those vertical wind tunnels that simulate a skydiving experience. The gunner told the pilot and had another gunner help drag the IO back into the airplane. On the way back to base, the following conversation occurred over the interphone.

IO: "Pilot, IO."
Pilot: "Go ahead."

IO: "Sir, that was fun. Can I do it again?"
Pilot: "You better **KEEP** your ass in this airplane!"

TIC with Our Grunts—This story is based on some facts that I'm aware of and supposedly takes place during the fighting at An Loc. The one thing that is historically correct is that AC-130s did indeed participate in that battle. In all fairness, it should be pointed out that this one engagement may have taken place elsewhere.

During my tour on gunships, we traditionally performed TICs with indigenous military units. More often than not, it was with Royal Laotian Army units with call signs like Red Onion, Green Onion, or Blue Onion. These were friendlies fighting against the North Vietnamese or the Pathet Lao. The Pathet Lao were Laotian communist fighters who were determined to overthrow the Laotian government. They were to Laos what the Viet Cong were to South Vietnam. But, in this one instance, the troops requesting support were our own. I don't recall the callsign for them, but for the purpose of this part of the story, we'll call the good guys "Cowboy." The initial contact went something like this.

"Any gunship, any gunship, this is Cowboy, over."

An AC-130 was on a mission nearby and heard the call. Not hearing a reply from any of the smaller gunships in country, the pilot came up on radio. The following conversations belie the fact that the guys on the ground never heard of an AC-130 or the callsign Spectre.

"Cowboy, this is 'any gunship', over."
"This is Cowboy. We're at [gives coordinates] and in need of immediate assistance, over."

"Roger, Cowboy. We copy and will be overhead in six minutes."
After approximately six minutes, "Cowboy, this is Spectre 02. We're on station and ready to copy request, over."

The grunts were only used to seeing an AC-47 at fifteen hundred feet and, seeing nothing ...

"Roger, Spectre 01. Are you sure of your position, over?"
"Roger, Cowboy. Start transmitting your request."
"We'll pop red smoke so you can identity."
We had a great system but it wasn't in color.
"We're pinned down at [coordinates] by 100+ bad guys in a long, rambling, concrete structure at our 12 o'clock. We'll begin our advance and need you to fire when they come out again."

At this point, the gunship crew realized that there was no AAA in the area and dropped down to F-altitude. That was the height for the 20 mms. The pilot instructed the gun crew to reset the 40s for F-altitude as well.

"Cowboy, do not, repeat, do not advance on that structure. We'll take care of it."

The #4 40 mm was on the line, and the pilot began firing at the building with no attempt to keep the rounds in one place. The building was struck multiple times with high-explosive rounds. With that, every bad guy in the building began rushing out. It resembled the results of pouring boiling water into an anthill.

(Highly excited voice) "What are you guys doing? They'll be all over us in a minute!"
"Cowboy, stand by, and keep your heads down."

By this time, the flight engineer and gunners had safed the 40 mm and armed both 20s. The pilot pressed the trigger twice, for three seconds each, and sent over five hundred rounds of high-explosive rounds into the target area. The attack essentially wiped out the entire enemy force.

"Spectre 02, this is Cowboy. They're all down. What do you guys got up there?"

"Never mind. What do you want next?"

While Cowboy took time to compose his answer, one of the sensor operators came on interphone and told the pilot that he found two Soviet-built tanks approaching the friendly's position at about one klick. The pilot immediately instructed the gunners to remove the HE from the 40 mm and load the armor-piercing incendiary (API).

"Cowboy, this is Spec 02."

"Spectre 02, go ahead."

"We've ID'd two T-62s about a klick east and heading your way."

"Holy *******! We see them and don't have a secure egress route. Thanks for your help, but we're done."

"Cowboy, duck!"

It took four rounds to destroy tank one and six to disable tank two.

"Spectre, the tanks are on fire and exploding. What the hell do you guys got up there?"

"Never mind. What's next?"

"Nuthin. We own the place. I want your guys' names and addresses. You're going to have the best Christmas ever!"

"Sorry, can't do that. Bye."

Friendly Fire—One of the toughest jobs in the Southeast Asia theater was the task of keeping aircraft separated. This was essential, given that nearly every aircraft carried things that went boom. There was the additional hazard of having hundreds of airplanes airborne at the same time, with altitudes ranging from just a few feet off the ground up to forty thousand feet. One of the frequent calls we heard at night was the "heavy arty" (heavy artillery) calls. The first time I heard that, I assumed that some artillery fire base was going to start lobbing shells near us. At our altitude, how bad could that be? The reality was a little different. "Heavy arty" was the code phrase for a B-52, or "Arc Light," strike. Having loaded bombs on these behemoths in Okinawa, I knew that the standard B-52 load for Southeast Asia was 108, five-hundred-pound bombs. I *knew* how bad that could be.

When in an orbit, attacking a convoy, a lot of triple-A comes up. You generally relax after striking your target and flying straight and level again. There were hundreds of turboprop aircraft flying round Southeast Asia, and most of them did not represent a threat to the enemy. They were either cargo or STOL aircraft. That being the case, we never took any ground fire when we were between targets. But, most of our IOs never took anything for granted and remained on the ramp as long as we were across the fence. This would prove to be a lifesaver for one crew.

The crew was between targets and flying straight and level. The gunners used this time to clean up around their guns, shovel brass, and have a smoke. Out of nowhere, the IO's voice yelled into the interphone for a violent, "Break right." The pilot obliged, and most of the gunners were knocked to the floor without warning. The IO finally called for the pilot to roll out, and the airplane was level once again. The flight deck crew and the gunners looked out windows and gun ports to see where the Triple-A was. Not seeing any, most assumed it was 57 mm being fired, as not all of 57 was tracer. The pilot asked the IO what was going on, and the IO directed the pilot to fly parallel to their original ground track but about a mile to the right of it. The IO then said to look at the ground of the original track. Several hundred explosions were occurring for about two miles along their original path. The crew looked upward to see three contrails in the moonlight at very high altitude. Hanging off the ramp, the IO saw the first explosions at their 6 o'clock and knew exactly what it was before calling for the break. It was a B-52 strike, and no one had transmitted the heavy arty call. Had the IO been off the ramp, the entire airplane would have been blanketed with five-hundred-pound bombs.

If there were a safety investigation of that incident, no one ever heard of it, or it was stuffed away somewhere, never to see the light of day. But that wasn't surprising during that period. It seemed to happen quite often. Although the incident was never talked about officially, it certainly was, in hushed tones, among the Spectre crew members of the time.

The Bomb—As we've already discussed, the rainy-season mission could really try your patience. Boredom and cold were the norm, and you'd do anything to liven up the party. One gun crew did just that one night. They grabbed a 40 mm ammo can and removed the interior spacers. The IO took an MK-24 out of the launcher and set the mechanism so that it would ignite in several minutes rather than immediately after launch. The Mk 24 was placed vertically in the center of the ammo can, and four cans of hydraulic fluid were placed between the can and the flare. That was meant to stabilize the flare and provide more bang for the buck when needed. Several rounds of 40 mm ammo were placed atop the hydraulic fluid cans, and one Mk-6 flare was placed on top. Three or four feet of linked 20 mm ammo were draped around the top of the whole thing to tie it together. The entire unit now weighed well over one hundred pounds, and it took two people to drag it to the edge of the ramp. The IO triggered the delay on the Mk 24 and placed his finger in the ring at the end of the lanyard of the Mk-6. His job was to hold on tight, while the gunners pushed the device off the ramp. The tug of the lanyard nearly dragged the IO off the ramp and into oblivion.

Having successfully ejected their cargo, the gunners and IO waited patiently for the small flash of light they expected on the ground. Two minutes passed, and they began to think their invention was a dud. The Mk-24 should have ignited by then, and the MK-6 started burning as soon as the lanyard was pulled. About the time they were about to admit to failure, a huge explosion and fireball erupted from the ground, about five to ten miles behind the aircraft. It looked like a small tactical nuke went off, and the radios started to come alive. This occurred over Laos, and aircraft over Vietnam began calling ABCCC to find out what was going on in area 14. The gunners and IO put on faces that mimicked little boys caught with their fingers in the cookie jar. The pilot was like a knowing mother and came on interphone. "Okay, gunners, knock it off."

The following account *is* true but seemingly belongs in the urban legends section. There were few amenities in the AC-130. Crew comfort was not a major issue for a mission that lasted an average of five hours. We had a coffee jug filled with the world's worst coffee and cardstock cups that would disintegrate and dump their contents onto you within five minutes. There was a urinal that was interesting, to say the least. It was a standard aircraft urinal top fitted to the right aft fuselage. From the bottom of the cup, a flex tube was snaked through the fuselage to a rearward pointing pitot tube. When used, the liquid would flow out the bottom of the urinal and be dissipated by the slipstream as it reached the outside world. On early models, the flare launcher was not always installed. This allowed the IOs to lie on the right-hand side of the ramp. They learned to avoid that side after several of them found themselves enveloped in a nasty yellow cloud.

As for "number 2," there were no provisions to accommodate that type of relief. After all, the missions only lasted five hours. Besides, we were always admonished to take care of that issue before we left the squadron and got on the bus. Well, not everyone has the same constitution as his peers, and Montezuma's revenge was always a threat if you ate downtown. We found that the 40 mm ammo can was a perfect height for sitting, and many were used for that purpose. Additionally, once used, you could put the top back on the can, which hermetically sealed it. Once sealed, you just tossed it off the ramp. I always thought about some poor local who found one of those things and took it home to use as a container or for some other use. There have to be hundreds of these treasures still lying around near the Ho Chi Minh Trails. Some archeologist, a few hundred years from now, will have a hard time figuring out that one.

CHAPTER 15

✪

OUR BIG, THEIR BIGGER

Except for missions, we rarely spent very much time at the squadron. So we always felt it rather odd when we were summoned for some type of briefing other than commander's call. Shortly before the E-models began arriving, all the gunners were scheduled to attend a classified meeting in the squadron briefing room. On arrival, we noted the speaker was an air force major, wearing his blue suit. That was a rare sight in the squadron building, as flight suits and jungle fatigues were the norm. This gentleman was apparently from some AF R&D or procurement unit. He was there to brief us on the new gun that would be mounted on the new E-models some two or three months after they arrived. The new gun was to be the 105 mm Howitzer. There were raised eyebrows in the room but no outward shock. All of us had seen so many bizarre applications to the AC-130 that nothing seemed inconceivable any more. The mounting was to be simple: the #4 40 mm gun would be removed, and the 105 placed in the left paratroop door. The new gun would be fitted to a hydraulically operated mount, which would have the ability to be tweaked by the fire control computer for miniscule corrections. Another notable fact about the new weapon and hydraulic mount was that the gun had a barrel extender installed. This addition made the barrel so long that the gun had to be raised before landing, or it would strike the runway before the landing gear. Without the hydraulic system, this would be impossible. As the major continued with his briefing, he regaled us with the tale of how he came to acquire the technical manuals for the gun. Obviously, a Howitzer isn't a standard air force weapon, so the tech data had to be acquired from the army. He was given the phone number of some army officer who was in charge of such matters and called him one evening. The number was to the army officer's billet, and given the music and loud voices in the background, there was obviously a party going on that included alcohol. After ensuring that he had the correct person, our major asked how he could acquire several copies of the manuals for the 105 mm Howitzer field piece. The army officer wanted to know why the air force was interested in a Howitzer. Our man explained that the air force was going to mount it in an aircraft and fire it. The major could hear the army officer's hand close over the phone's mouthpiece, and he yelled to his guests that some air force idiot wanted to mount a 105 on an airplane and shoot it. It took about two minutes for the laughing, jokes, and intellect insults to simmer down, but our guy finally convinced the army gent that the request was quite real and convinced him to send the manuals. The rest, as they say, is history.

The summer and fall of 1971 saw some major upgrades for both sides. R&D and technical advances were the course of action on our side, whereas bigger, more lethal weapon systems were their theme.

As pointed out in previous chapters, the bad guys had their share of all types of antiaircraft artillery. Although moderately successful, they didn't have as much of an impact on US aircraft as they would have liked. And, since the Soviet Union never had a problem supplying arms to their communist satellites throughout the world, they were more than happy to help out with this new problem. One of the newer weapons exported by the Soviets was the SA-7 "Strela" surface-to-air missile. (Today's upgraded version is called the Grail.) This was a shoulder-fired, heat-seeking device that, although somewhat crude for its time, could ruin the day of any low-flying aircraft. It could fly at nearly thirteen hundred miles an hour and had a 2.5-pound warhead. Adding to the fact that we flew well within its fourteen thousand–foot max altitude, this was an obvious threat, and we took it seriously. Although generally feared for the possibility of merely damaging one of our huge airplanes, it was one of those that was responsible for the downing of an AC-130 in 1972. However, another Soviet weapon system had been around since the late 1950s and was the cause of serious amounts of grief within the gunship world. Our first briefing of the new threat caused eyes as big as pie plates throughout the room. This was the SA-2 Guideline, SAM. This monster was nearly forty-feet long, had a four-hundred-pound warhead, came at you at Mach III, and was responsible for downing Francis Gary Powers' U-2 in 1960. It is a two-stage missile that incorporated a solid fuel booster and a liquid fuel sustainer. When launched at night, there wasn't a doubt in your mind what was coming, because the initial blast of the solid booster ignition resembles a napalm canister detonation. Given that this was a very large missile with a great deal of sensitive electronics, no one would have guessed that it could be successfully transported down the Ho Chi Minh Trail and used effectively. By today's standards, it would be similar to dropping your PC down a flight of stairs and having it operate as if nothing happened. This was one time we must give the enemy credit where credit is due. As was the case with the Strela, the SA-2 was also a crew killer and responsible for another AC-130 loss in 1972.

On our side, the gunship program was becoming a superstar to the boys in Washington. One of our staunchest supporters was President Nixon himself. His favorite duty during the workweek was to watch the BDA films from Spectre on Fridays. We had a rudimentary videotape recording system on the airplane that recorded exactly what we saw during an attack. These tapes were transferred to film and sent directly to the White House for viewing by the commander in chief. Due to our success, it was inevitable that a follow-on AC-130 model would be the next logical step. After all, the A-models were all built in the early fifties and were getting old. It was rumored that there were no A-models at Ubon that didn't have a red X in their maintenance logs for cracked main wing spars. The most numerous cargo-hauling version of the Hercules at this time was the

C-130E, which made it the obvious candidate. By early fall of 1971, we got the news that the E-model was in fact to become the follow-on model and that the first one was due shortly. When the first one arrived at Ubon, the only visible difference was that the E-model had four-bladed props, whereas the A-model had only three. The rest of the differences were only made apparent if you were tagged to fly in it. The missions in the A-model averaged four and a half hours. The E-model averaged six. We used to joke about the thing making its own fuel as it flew. The E-model was also faster than the A. Probably a good thing when trying to run away from big guns and big missiles. But, for some reason, the longer blades of the A-model allowed it to climb and turn better. This fact became moot many years later, when all the remaining A-models were refitted with four-blade props. Fortunately, the few E-models we acquired before I left for the States were predominately flown by the crews that trained on them before their delivery to Thailand. That was fine with the rest of us, as we felt the four- to five-hour missions in the A-model were long enough.

Note: Although the airframe never drastically changed, the E-model was eventually redesignated the H-model, and some of these are still flying today with the 16th SOS at Canon Air Force Base, New Mexico.

CHAPTER 16

✪

CRITTERS AND PARTY SUITS

Nearly every military outfit in the world has its share of mascots and distinctive items of clothing that are special to their unit. For flying units, most of the mascots were represented by nose art on their aircraft. Looking back to WWII, one can find a plethora of eagles, owls, boxing chickens, and billy goats. The AC-130 didn't have animals as their nose art. Rather, we used ghostly and spectral images designed to replicate real and imagined death in its most horrible form. We *did*, however, have our animals. The "official" one derived from the affectionate term given to the C-130 by just about everyone. As it's a big, lumbering, and not so graceful aircraft, it was always referred to as a turkey. Believe it or not, we really didn't mind, as it was always said with affection. With that in mind, the squadron got itself a live turkey as a mascot. Normally, one would think that the care and feeding of such a bird would automatically be the job of some poor enlisted slob. Not in this case. The 16th SOS designated a new position within the squadron. The official title of this position was TCO, the turkey control officer. And the position would be filled by the lowest-ranking second lieutenant in the unit. Initially, we enlisted folks thought the concept was funny as hell, as did everyone else. But it could occasionally get silly to the point of rage. Each time we got word that new crew members were about to arrive from the States, the TCO would hurry over to the terminal to see if any second lieutenants were among the group. If there were, the new guy was forced to state his date of rank (DOR). If it was newer than the current TCO's DOR, the new guy became the new TCO. If the dates were the same, the tie was broken by the date of service, which was usually within a few days of each other. Sometimes, it almost got to the point of paper-rock-scissors.

Before speaking of the next critter, the story of the party suit must be told. Although it almost never happened on the bases in the United States, overseas units usually had some form of uniform or clothing items that set them apart from the other units. At Ubon, we had the party suit. These were essentially flight suits that were made from black cotton fabric and adorned with numerous unofficial patches of every variety, along with the standard wings and the person's name over the left breast. The majority of the patches were of an individual's choosing and ran the gamut from humor to serious. One of my favorites was an embroidered AC-130 on a patch with the words, "Fabulous Four-Engined Fighters of the Wolf Pack." Wolf Pack was the name given to the 8th Tactical Fighter Wing (TFW), of which the 16th SOS was a part. The wording was very special due to an incident that made the fighter units of the 8th TFW cringe with envy. The first hostile aircraft shot down by an 8th TFW aircraft was not by an F-4. Rather, this remarkable feat was accomplished by an early AC-130 that took out a North Vietnamese helicopter while on a daylight mission. Therein lays the genesis of the phrase, "Fabulous Four-Engined Fighters."

There were also patches that had a semi-official significance to them and had to be earned. The most cherished was the "Battle Damaged Qualified" patch. In the movie *The Right Stuff,* a young lady inquires about the pictures of test pilots on the wall behind the bar. She asks what a pilot had to do to get their picture hung there. The answer was that he had to die. The criteria for being awarded a Battle Damaged Qualified patch was nearly the same. In order to get one, you had to be in an airplane that took a direct hit by enemy antiaircraft fire. Another patch that was kinda/sorta cherished by the officers has its roots in the job description of the gunner manning the 20 mm Vulcans. As stated earlier in the book, the brass had to be shoveled off the floor and into duffel bags. This tended to be back-breaking work, and we loved it when someone else volunteered to help. This was especially true when we went Winchester on the 20 mm ammo, and three thousand cases and links were scattered all over the floor. One mustn't forget that it would be tiring on the ground. But we had to do it in an unpressurized airplane at nearly ten thousand feet, where the air is pretty thin, and occasionally in a pylon turn pulling extra Gs. Even when you're twenty-something and in good physical condition, this activity can wear you out in short order. I exchanged e-mails with our crew's BC operator, Major Ed Wakeman, and he has one of these patches. It is one of his more treasured items from that assignment. He has graciously donated it to the Air Force Museum at Wright-Patterson AFB.

Needless to say, even something as trivial as our party suits were very important to us. You wore it any time you were off duty and nearly always to informal squadron social functions. As mentioned in the "Spectre Urban Legends" chapter, we weren't very popular among the other enlisted at the base, and this was quite evident if we walked the base wearing a party suit. On some occasions, it was as if we were wearing a bull's-eye on our backs. But, things got even worse after a few months. Our Intel people informed us that there was a US five-figure bounty on us. The North was facing severe shortages in their campaign below the DMZ, and Spectre was the main culprit. All they knew was a callsign, the sound of turboprop engines, and the fact that their equipment and supplies were being very accurately decimated on the Ho Chi Minh Trails. The reward was to be given to anyone who turned in one of us or otherwise pointed us out to the bad guys. Now, it must be understood that the Thais hate the commies. They always have and they always will. But, when your annual income is the equivalent of about $800 a year, five digits sounds pretty appealing. The figure I "heard," but cannot confirm, was US$25,000. And since so many of our group lived on the local economy, the base commander ruled that we were no longer to wear our party suits off base. Surprisingly, not too many of us balked at that directive. After all, who wants to be kidnapped, or worse?

Now that I have described the party suits and their meaning, I can move on to critter #2. Back in chapter 9, I referred to Lieutenant Colonel Harris, our squadron commander. His nickname was "Grouchy Bear," or "GB" for short. One of our IOs had a pet gibbon he called GeeBee. The ape became more famous than the turkey, possibly due to his name or possibly because the IO had a miniature Spectre party suit made for the little guy. Over the left breast pocket were a set of embroidered enlisted aircrew wings and the letters GB where the name was normally found.

There was a squadron picnic one day, and we did the usual fare with hamburgers, hot dogs, and beer. Tending the beer keg on this occasion was this particular IO and GB. At one point, Colonel Harris and the Ops officer, Lieutenant Colonel George Fox, joined us and came to the keg for a glass of brew. Colonel Harris was in a jovial mood and told Colonel Fox that the gibbon looked just like him. The Ops officer replied that the GB didn't stand for George Fox. I'd been in the air force for over three years, and that's the first inkling I'd had that officers actually had a sense of humor and a willingness to pick on one another. I'd obviously had a very cloistered career up to that point.

CHAPTER 17

★

THE LAND OF SMILES

Thailand is referred to as, "the land of smiles." But it has not always been so. History shows that the name "Thailand" is relatively new. The original name of this beautiful country was Siam. Its true pronunciation is "see-YAHM." Its history is as colorful as it is long: nearly four thousand years. As with most of Asia, the Thai people have their roots in China, although some of their culture is derived from the Khmer who invaded Thailand some thousands of years ago. Over a period of years, these Chinese descendants migrated into what is known today as Southeast Asia. These people included present-day Thai, Laotians, Burmese, Cambodian, and Vietnamese. Thailand borders all these counties except Vietnam and most generally got along with most. Throughout history, however, it seems that Burma, now referred to by some as Myanmar, has been a thorn in Thailand's side. There have been constant border clashes, dating back a very long time. The most recent clash of note was in 2001. Thailand and Laos have had their share of disagreements, too, but to a much lesser extent than with Burma. In fact, the Thai and Lao cultures are very close in structure and language; even their alphabets look very similar. There were a great deal of Laotians living and working in Thailand during the Vietnam War, and most Americans couldn't tell the difference. There are a lot of American servicemen who married women from Thailand, but the majority of them are ethnic Lao.

On leaving the confines of the base, one still did not see the "real" Thailand. As with military bases all over the world, the city situated next to a military installation will, inevitably, retool its economy in deference to its national and foreign military servicemen. It's true in the United States, and it's true in Thailand. Nearly every merchant has signs hawking his products or services in Thai and English. However, even the up-country Thai cities and towns manage to maintain some of their cultural history and flair. Ubon is no exception. The parks, smaller shops, temples, and railway stations are still as quaint and culturally correct as they had been for centuries. An hour's drive out of Ubon is what is commonly referred to as the Big Buddha. The Thais are most generally Buddhist, with a sprinkling of Christians and Muslims. The Big Buddha was supposedly the largest statue of its kind in Southeast Asia and was relatively new when I went to see it in 1971. Also in the compound were stone Buddha images that were about two to four feet high and reported to be over one thousand years old. An interesting observation I made was the way Buddha is represented by the different Asian countries. The Japanese Buddha is very round faced and stoic looking. The Chinese version is rather corpulent and happy. But the Thai version is svelte, graceful, and has the air of decency and enlightenment. And since the word "Buddha" means "the awakened or enlightened one," the image seems appropriate. And being a product of the land of smiles, the Thai Buddha always wears a slight, knowing smile.

Bangkok is not only the capital of Thailand, it is a totally different story from the up country cities. Even in 1971, it was (and is) one of the most Westernized cities in Southeast Asia. It's a low-lying city that's ringed with rivers and *klongs* (canals). Although there was a plethora of public transportation, many of the residents had cars. Prior to traveling to Thailand, the only place I had seen that much vehicle congestion was in Montreal. The streets of Bangkok were so congested that the traffic cops sat in enclosures atop large poles at the intersections.

Bangkok is a foodie's paradise. Just about every cuisine imaginable is available in that sprawling city. And surprisingly, some of the best was available on the klongs. That area of Bangkok resembles Venice with a Thai accent. Small canoe-like craft are slowly rowed along the lengths of the canals. They are generally operated by women, the bravest of whom offer freshly cooked food. These vessels have a Thai version of a hibachi sitting on the floor of the boat. When you place your order, either a wire grid or container of oil for frying is set on the fire, and you watch as your meal is prepared. This is generally done boat to boat, but they will also serve shore-bound customers. The other floating marketers sell everything from fresh fruit and vegetables to cuts of meats and eggs. There's a saying about the eating habits of the locals in Shanghai, China. They'll eat anything that flies, except an airplane, and anything with four legs, except a table. If Shanghai is the leader in that category, Bangkok comes in a close second.

In 1971, the Bangkok Zoo probably couldn't have been described as "world class." But, it had enough unusual critters to make it a worthwhile stop during a visit to Bangkok.

CHAPTER 18

✪

THE THAI MILITARY

One night in 1971, several sappers eluded the perimeter guards and found their way onto the base at Ubon. Their mission: damage or destroy as many gunships as possible. However, they were confronted by one major problem. When Hanoi issued the op order for the attack, the only gunships they were aware of were the AC-47 Spookys. The C-130 was known only as a transport and not worth the effort. So, our Gomers crept right past all the Spectres and proceeded to the transient ramp in front of base ops. This is where visiting aircraft were temporarily parked. Arriving there, our intrepid sappers proceeded to blow the shit out of a lone C-47 trash hauler that was from off station and parked there for the night. Within thirty seconds of the explosion, an American jeep appeared with an M-60 mounted on it. The jeep's gunner dispatched two or three bad guys immediately, but another got away and ran toward the main gate. I've always found that to be an unusual act on the part of the sapper, as the gate was on the opposite end of the runway, had armed guards, and led right into the middle of downtown Ubon. Had he gone the same way he came in, he would have had the cover of darkness and the jungle at the end of the runway. The sapper's route of egress was radioed to the main gate and acknowledged. Just about that time, a Thai guard appeared from the gatehouse and ran toward the area where the sapper should be. The sapper had the misfortune to pop out of the grass just as the guard arrived. I use the word "misfortune," as the Thai guard proceeded to pump an entire thirty-round banana clip's worth of bullets into the bad guy. Another version of the same story had the Thai guard using *two* banana clips, but I find that unlikely. Anyway, 'nuff said.

If you were to look at a political map of Southeast Asia today, and the countries under communist rule were colored red, you would see an island of white surrounded by a sea of red. That island is Thailand. To the west is communist Myanmar. To the north and east is communist Laos. And, to the extreme east is communist Vietnam. Some will argue that the main reason for this is Thailand's close relationship with the United States. Although this idea may be based in a modicum of fact, the real reason is that the Thais want no part of communism and have hated the concept since its inception. The Thai government is a constitutional monarchy, similar to Great Britain. The major difference is that not all Brits love and adore their queen. A minority would even like to see the monarchy in Britain abolished completely. Not so in Thailand. Their king, Buhimol Adulyadej (pronounced poo-me-pon ah-dune-yah-det), is loved and revered by his people more than any current monarch. Although the king is only a figurehead within the government, the Thai prime minister must knee walk into the king's presence for any form of consultation or meeting. The reason for bringing up these facts will be made clear in the following portions of the story.

The Thai Border Patrol—This group of true Thai patriots is commanded and partially manned by the Thai military. But the remainder is comprised of folks that will do anything asked of them to preserve the country's independence and monarchy. Even the lowliest, hardened criminal in Thailand loves the king and would do anything for him. And that is exactly where recruitment is done. When the Border Patrol needs more men, they go to the prisons and interview inmates under sentence of death for their crimes. In a country where the median yearly income equals a week's pay in the United States, a person can be murdered for $10. In the interview process, the inmate is asked if he knows he's under penalty of death, that the sentence will be carried out soon, if they hate commies, if they love their king, and would do anything asked of them on his behalf. The answer is nearly always a resounding yes. After careful screening, these people become part of the Border Patrol. Their life, although spared, is no cakewalk. They walk the entire border of Thailand and watch for any incursion. There's an old adage that goes, "Shoot first and ask questions later." The Border Patrol always shoots first and never has any questions. Anyone observed crossing their border from a neighboring country will be shot dead. Not stopped, not questioned, just dead. It's as simple as that.

The Royal Thai Air Force—The Thai military isn't as unforgiving as their Border Patrol contemporaries. But that doesn't mean they are ignored. They are a very well trained and lethal fighting force. At Ubon, we had our share of American security police providing guard duties and patrolling the perimeter fences. But it was still a Royal Thai Air Force Base, and they were in charge. Our "cops" had standard M-16s with standard twenty-round magazines. The Thai guards also had M-16s but with a thirty-round banana clip and have no problem using it.

CHAPTER 19

✪

PROMETHEUS

If the old saying, "If it weren't for bad luck, I'd have no luck at all," were turned into nose art, it surely would have appeared on AC-130 tail #044. As history correctly points out, the nickname for this airplane was, in fact, *Prometheus*. We had a penchant for naming our airplanes after mythological characters with powerful, warrior-like qualities, or some other form of snarling, "get even," entity. Prometheus was a character from Greek mythology and had quite a story in his own right. He was brother to Atlas and was also a Titan. He stole fire from Zeus and gave it to mortal man. This was a crime, and he was punished by Zeus in a most horrible way. Somehow, the stories of the Greek Titan and tail #044 are a bit too closely interlinked.

On a November night in 1971, *Prometheus* took off on a routine mission. The flight was pretty boring until about 1:45 in the morning. The entire crew felt and heard a loud thump. This was unusual, as they were flying straight and level and not rolled in on a target. Sparks and a ball of fire were reported going past the right side of the aircraft by crew members in the back. But looking at the engine instruments, the pilot, Captain Charles Baertl, noted that all the instruments indicated normal engine operation. The only thing different was the aircraft had lost two thousand feet of altitude. The aircraft *did* seem to yaw a bit to the right, and throttle movement for the right-hand engines didn't seem to have an effect, so the pilot decided to feather the props. After that was accomplished, the flight engineer went back to take a look and discovered the props were missing on the number 3 and 4 engines.

The aircraft was eventually flown back to Ubon, and a landing was made, albeit with great difficulty. The crew survived, and it was left to the flight engineer to sum up the event. He stated, "Gentlemen, that was a routine two-engine landing."

It didn't take long for the maintenance people to find the cause of the accident. A turboprop is, essentially, a jet engine driving a propeller. The propeller speed is reduced from the 10,000 rpm that the jet engine turns by a gear reduction mechanism that is not totally unlike the transmission of a car. The output shaft from the transmission to the propeller is called a torque tube. The tube is actually two tubes, one inside the other. The difference between the engine's torque and the torque to the propeller is measured by sensors connected to the system and displayed to the pilots and flight engineer. The problem occurred when the torque tube on engine #3 suddenly seized, causing the propeller cluster to stop abruptly. If a helicopter loses one of its rotor blades while the blades are turning, the blade can be thrown as far as five miles. And its blades are turning at less than 100 rpm. The propeller on a turboprop, at cruise setting, is spinning at well in excess of 1,000 rpm. When a several-thousand-pound propeller stops abruptly, the energy has to go someplace. In this instance, the pent-up energy caused the propeller to snap off the engine, heading outboard like a combat Frisbee, taking the #4 propeller with it. The crew was indeed lucky, as had the propeller traveled inboard, it would have cut the fuselage in half, just in front of the right scanner.

The airplane was eventually repaired and flew combat missions for another four months. However, *Prometheus* was shot down in March of 1972, and the entire crew was lost. It was the first of three gunships to be lost that year. The crew's remains were finally discovered after nearly forty years and interred at Arlington National Cemetery in June of 2010. Rest in peace, gentlemen.

Update: Prior to the initial release of this story, no one had a definitive explanation as to what caused the propellers to leave the engines that night. However, since the first publication of the book in Apr 2011, a surviving crew member from the incident has been located and interviewed by phone. The aircraft was indeed being fired at. There's a possibility that the North may have been transporting 57 MM AAA rounds fitted with with proximity fuses to their units along the Trail. This suggests a possibility for the damage incurred by Prometheus. This type of fuse detects a metallic mass as it flies through the air and detonates the warhead when the proximity is at its closest point. No one confirmed this type of round actually did the damage but there were shrapnel fragments found in the wing and the final report apparently stated antiaircraft fire as the culprit. Still, a great deal of speculation surrounds the incident to this day.

CHAPTER 20

✪

THE RESCUE ATTEMPT

Anyone with memories of the Vietnam conflict remembers the failed rescue attempt of American POWs in the Son Tay prison camp in November of 1970. The planning and execution of the attempt were flawless. The attempt failed because all the POWs had been moved shortly before the attempt was made. This was not the only attempt to free POWs during the Vietnam war.

One night in 1971, our crew assembled at the squadron to prepare for our truck-hunting mission that night. We were taken aside by some senior wing staff officers and told to stand by in the briefing room. Eventually, we were joined by the wing intelligence branch chief and some plainclothesmen, who could have been anyone from the CIA to the Defense Intelligence Agency. This wasn't uncommon, as we were occasionally joined by these folks for any number of reasons. But this night was different. The security was the tightest I'd ever seen. The initial briefing was to the effect that a POW rescue attempt was being made somewhere in the boonies. But, they wouldn't tell us anything more until some additional intel had been received and other resources were in place. Even after telling us that little bit, we weren't allowed to leave the briefing room unescorted for fear of someone forgetting himself and discussing the mission outside of a secure room. Every now and again, we'd be told some additional little bits and pieces of what was supposed to happen. There seemed to be an air of panic when it was learned that our airplane was suffering some maintenance problem. Our question then became, "Why don't we just use a different airplane?" This is when the seriousness of the operation began to play itself out to us, the crew. We suspected that the security was so tight because something special may have been added to the airplane. The two things we did find out was that the entire operation hinged on our airplane and that the timing was so critical that we had a very narrow window of opportunity to perform the mission. It had to happen within that window and could not be moved up, back, or rescheduled. If we weren't over a particular point of ground at a particular time, the entire effort would be scrubbed. The maintenance on our aircraft became overwhelming and couldn't be completed within the given time frame. The mission was canceled, and we were given a security debrief the likes of which I never saw again until my time dealing with nuclear weapons in B-52s. To this day, I have no idea who was in the camp, what their nationality was or where it was located. The navigator wasn't even going to be given the charts until engine start, and it was clear no one could get off or on the airplane.

The only conclusion I can make after all these years was that it probably wasn't going to occur in Vietnam and that the POWs might not be Americans. Even then, that's only speculation. I doubt that more than a handful of people knew precisely what the mission was about, and I'm sure they're not talking.

Of all the missions I flew in the AC-130, that was the only one in which I had a genuine feeling of utter disappointment and sadness for not having flown.

CHAPTER 21

✪

GOING HOME

In the TV series *M*A*S*H,* I was always taken by the fact that Hotlips and Frank Burns worried about only one major issue: the status of the peace talks. They would inevitably become upset when the talks went well, because the possibility of the end of the war also signaled the end of their war-long love affair. They would uses phrases like, "The war can't last forever," or, "All good things must come to an end." Initially, I saw the humor the writers were trying to convey. But, looking back, I find that I went through a little of that myself. As explained earlier, the gunship program was a one-of-a-kind mission, and once you left it, you would go back to whatever you did before Spectre. It didn't matter if you were heading back for separation, as was my case, or being reassigned to a base in the States. You knew that you would probably never see the people you flew with again and that whatever your new duty was, it couldn't hold a candle to what you did over the past year. All you would have are your memories, and you would not be allowed to share them with anyone not associated with the gunship program. When my turn came for rotation back to the world, I was forced to learn what "mixed emotions" actually meant.

My last official flight was on October 29, with tail #509. My friend Joel, from Castle, and I had been at Ubon for nearly a year and shared the same bungalow off base. However, we never got to fly together. By special request, we did so on my last flight, as it was his last one as well. We were still in the final throes of the rainy season, and the mission was dull and boring. Neither side fired a shot, and we landed with our full ammo compliment intact. It was a sort of belly drop for one's last night in combat. But, who knows? Perhaps it was meant to be so that I could write this book.

November of 1971 saw me wrestling with more emotions and decisions than is moral for a twenty-three-year-old. Part of the drill was to begin winding down the flying and performing some less exciting duties. The gunners had the job of meeting returning flights with trailers filled with ammo for replenishment. We would remove the brass and links and fill the airplane with a fresh load of ammo. I had the misfortune of removing a stuck trailer tongue from the pickup we used to haul the trailer from place to place. The donut ring of the trailer tongue was wedged into the hook of the truck. I pulled up with all my might but couldn't release it. I told one of the other guys to jump in and release the brake. When he did, the pressure was released. With me still pulling upward, the tongue—which, by the way, weighed in excess of one hundred pounds—shot straight up and then down again, landing on my foot and breaking a toe. I got on my motorcycle and drove to the hospital. I came out with a half cast that included a thick, rubber doohickey on the bottom for walking. I felt lucky, as the broken toe was on the foot I used on the bike's brake pedal instead of the foot I used on the bike's gear shift pedal. It took me an extra minute to position the crutches across the seat so I could sit on them and then I headed downtown to my bungalow. Riding a motorcycle with a cast on your foot isn't a great idea, and I had to have the cast replaced on the third day. Seems I missed the brake pedal a few times with the rubber doohickey.

During my stay at Ubon, I recall reading an article in the *Stars and Stripes* titled "What Price DFC?" The DFC is the Distinguished Flying Cross and is one of the most highly coveted decorations that can be awarded to a flyer. That's what brought my attention to the article. It seems as if there were some clerk-typists in Vietnam who were gaming the system. They knew the promotion system well, since they were the ones who typed up all the citations. A couple of them had duties requiring them to occasionally fly from Base X to Base Y in-country. Since the flight was over a combat zone, they'd put themselves in for the DFC and actually got them. Those of us who received DFCs and Air Medals did so in aerial combat and felt we'd earned them. The thought of these people wearing them under false pretenses was despicable and cheapened the decorations we'd earned honestly. That brings me to the next point. Our wing had a policy in which the combat flyers who simply weren't at the right place at the right time could put in for a DFC if they didn't already have one. After all, these guys did what the rest of us had done and were in just as much jeopardy as we were. Most of the time, they were unlucky enough to have a DFC request downgraded to an Air Medal by higher headquarters. For whatever reason, they simply never got noticed. The decoration was referred to as an End of Tour DFC. The applicant could choose a mission that was particularly special, and the award was just about a 100 percent guarantee. Although the policy was directed at the folks who never got the award, any crew member was entitled to one. When asked if I would put in for one, I declined. In my year there, I had already been awarded two DFCs and nine Air Medals. I say this with respect and admiration for the guys who didn't get noticed, but I didn't feel the need for a freebie. Perhaps the earlier *Stars and Stripes* article poisoned me. I can't be certain. But, after seeing the "stolen honor" thieves who are out there today, I know now I'm satisfied with my decision. Because one of these nimrods was recently discovered in the Spectre Association, the executive board was forced to convene and write an addendum to the by-laws that directs expulsion for these thieves.

One of the more sinister aspects of air force life was its promotion system. In addition to decorations, time in grade, time in service, and performance reports, we were required to take two written tests. One was designed to have you compete with every other person in your grade in the air force. It was a test of general military knowledge based on rank. Another written test pitted those of the same specialty and same rank against each other. Both tests were worth one hundred points each. The other promotion considerations, listed previously, had a maximum number of points assigned to them. You tested, and the air force came up with some algorithm that assigned a cutoff score for each specialty. You had to score at or above the cutoff to be promoted. I was a buck sergeant when I arrived at Ubon and had taken the tests back in May or June. At some point in September or October, I received a letter from the personnel people, informing me that my test results were lost or otherwise unusable, and I would have to retest. A sweet gesture, but since I was getting out in two months, I declined. The promotions are always released on the first day of the month, and having declined the retest, I had no reason to expect anything. But, every day I went to a particular filing cabinet in the squadron and checked to see if I had any paperwork. It seemed odd that I never did, especially when I was getting so close to my DEROS. Then, in the second or third week in November, one of the guys came up to me and started pumping my hand. He congratulated me on making staff sergeant. I didn't consider it a particularly funny joke and told him so. He said that it was no joke and that I should check my crew folder. I explained that I just did, and there was nothing in there for me. He essentially took me by the hand to the filing cabinet and opened a drawer marked "Temp," or "Out Processing," or something of that nature. Inside, I discovered about twelve pages of paperwork for me, including one that promoted me to staff sergeant. The first words out of my mouth should have been words of joy and thanks, but I said, "Why the hell doesn't someone tell me about these things?" in reference as to why I had a crew folder change and was never notified about it. After a minute or so, I made the appropriate happy happy, joy joy comments and all the thank you's I could muster. I'd been a staff sergeant longer than I had time left in the military and didn't even know it. I actually got to wear the extra stripe for another two and a half weeks. But, as I began to think about it, some serious implications came to light. In the air force, it was very difficult to make staff with fewer than four years of service, especially for the career field I was assigned to. This became a whole new ball of wax. In the weapons and munitions career field, the jump from buck sergeant to staff was huge. All kinds of career-building opportunities open up with that jump, not to mention the opportunities of day-to-day life. In one fell swoop, you transition from worker bee to middle manager, otherwise known as the day you start to get fat. Knowing all this, I had to find out what types of options I had. I had already done the paperwork to separate, and it was already approved. I went to the personnel office and asked about what options I had if I wanted to stay in. The good news was that it was possible. The bad news was that I'd have to remain at Ubon until January or February, as it would take that long to cancel my travel and separation orders and come up with a new plan as to where to send me next. Obviously, the decision process became more convoluted, and I had to do a lot of hard thinking in the next day or so. Two things prevented me from accepting their proposal. The first was personal and perhaps a little childish and self-centered: the thought of missing another Christmas at home didn't please me. There was also a girlfriend with whom I'd just begun a relationship with in the months preceding my arrival overseas. We were both interested in seeing where the relationship might be headed, and that's hard to do from twelve thousand miles away. The second issue was of a more serious nature and bordered on superstition. It seemed that if you stayed for a second combat tour, your chances of survival were dramatically reduced. The latter was dramatically shown to be true in the three airplanes that were shot down in 1972. One of the crew members who died was a fellow I'd been with all through training, starting with general survival school in Washington. His airplane was downed by an SA-2, in March of 1972. Another personal loss was a very dear friend of Dale's, who was lost to an SA-7 in June of that year. I remember that date very well, as it was on my birthday. I obviously didn't know about these facts in 1971, but my instincts told me to pass. So, on December 5, 1971, I boarded a C-141 and began the trip that would take me to Bangkok and Don Muang Airport. From there, it was on to a civilian charter airline to Travis AFB, California, and ultimately … home.

EPILOGUE

---⭐---

I did in fact separate on arriving at Travis. I returned to Canada to live near my parents and see where my life would take me. The economy up there in 1972 was not very good, and the job market was only outstanding for the proverbial ditch diggers. In March of 1973, I headed back to Buffalo and re-upped. I was able to come back in as a staff sergeant and headed to Castle AFB, California, for the second time. While in Ontario, I took flying lessons and got to within five hours of finishing and becoming licensed. I made up those hours with the Castle Aero Club and got my private pilot's license in the summer of 1973. After a couple of years of bomb loading, I realized how much I missed flying and cross-trained to become a B-52 gunner. Flying backward at six hundred miles per hour, with no window, was a tad different than crewing an AC-130. By the time I retired from Uncle Sugar's Air Force in 1989, I had amassed over three thousand hours in the B-52 and over one hundred combat missions in the AC-130. No offense to all you SAC guys, who I love and admire, but I wouldn't trade my Spectre time for love or money.

Earlier in the story, I mentioned how the *First Lady* and *Azreal* were still major players in my life today. That is because they are two of the few surviving AC-130As that are still intact and on display in major venues. *Azreal* is located in the United States Air Force Museum at Wright-Patterson AFB in Dayton, Ohio. The *First Lady* is on display at Eglin AFB, near Valparaiso, Florida. And, if I really wanted to push the envelope, I could select tail #509, *Raid Kills um Dead*, as it was the aircraft on which I flew my last mission, according to my flight records, and which is currently on display at Hurlburt Field, an annex of Eglin AFB.

These days, in my sixties, I look back at my time in Spectre and ask myself a lot of seemingly poignant questions. One of the most frequently asked has to do with the fact that being a crew member on a gunship was strictly voluntary, not to mention supremely dangerous. Why on earth would I have volunteered for such hazardous duty? I must have been out of my mind or suffered from some uncontrollable mental defect. I didn't do drugs (really), so that couldn't have been the cause. I don't recall hitting my head on anything, either. Perhaps Bill Cosby was right and it was "brain damage"! To date, the only answer I have for that question is a quick shrug. The next question, however, has always been more succinct and more quickly answered. Knowing what I know now about the gunship program, the hazards, and what I went through, would I do it again? The answer is unmistakable. In a heartbeat!

CONCLUSION

★

The original AC-130 program was a stopgap fix to the problem of supplies moving down the Ho Chi Minh Trail. No other military system ever came close to achieving the success rate Spectre achieved in that arena. Although designed as a truck killer, the AC-130 also proved itself an effective deterrent in the TIC roll.

There's one more major change to the gunship program that wasn't in place when I flew with them. In those days, you didn't really change your specialty code, and the assignment resembled a long-term TDY rather than a PCS. Once you left it, you probably wouldn't be doing that duty again, although there were some exceptions. In today's AC-130 program, that has all changed. The gunship squadrons are permanent duty, and the crew positions are now recognized career fields. Once you sign up, it's just like being a cook or a military pay specialist. You're in it for the duration.

Today's Spectre isn't really "Spectre" anymore. The newest model of AC-130, the AC-130U, has been given the nickname of *Spooky II*, in honor of the original fixed-wing gunship. Of the entire AC-130 family, *Spooky II* is the first truly dedicated production gunship. This means that *Spooky II* wasn't a conversion of an existing airframe, as was all its predecessors. Rather, it was built from the ground up as a gunship. It has new weapons and new onboard systems that make it incredibly versatile. It isn't just a truck killer, and it isn't just a TIC support airplane.

It does it all—and more—with the finesse and stealth of an armed, very dangerous ballerina wearing a gunship gray cloak. And, as was the case with its older relatives, if it shows up and you're the bad guy, you're going to simply go away.

GLOSSARY

AAA (or Triple A)—Antiaircraft Artillery

ABCCC—Airborne Command and Control Center

ADC—Aerospace Defense Command

BC—Black Crow

BDA—Battle Damage Assessment

Bingo Fuel—Little or no fuel remaining

Bofors—40 mm antiaircraft gun, originally designed by Sweden, placed in service in 1934

Bullseye—Term used by one aircraft to direct another to cease firing

CBU—Cluster Bomb Unit. Hollow, bomb-shaped canister, generally containing hundreds of sub-munitions or bomblets

Charlie—Phonetic alphabet for the letter C. Used to define (c)ommunists or Viet (C)ong

Christmas Tree—An aircraft with all its external and internal lights turned on

Dead Nuts—Theoretical center of the pylon turn

DMZ—Demilitarized Zone

E&E—Escape and Evasion

FAC—Forward Air Controller

Fast Mover—Jet fighter and attack aircraft

FCO—Fire Control Officer

Fence—Border between Thailand and Laos

Fire Base—Encampment or base equipped with artillery pieces used in support of ground forces

Gomer—Nickname given to communist enemy in Laos

HE—High Explosive

HEI—High-Explosive Incendiary

HEIT—High-Explosive Incendiary Tracer

Hillsborough—Daytime callsign for ABCCC

HUD—Heads-Up Display

Igloo—A concrete covered Quonset style structure, covered with several feet of soil and vegetation, and used to store weapons and explosives.

Incendiary—Material that when ignited, causes fire and serious burns

IO—Illuminator Operator

IR—Infrared

Jink – Abrupt horizontal and vertical position changes intended to complicate the aim of an attacker.

Klick (or Click)—Kilometer

kw—Kilowatt

LLTV—Low Light Level Television

LTV—Ling-Tempco-Vought: an electronics supplier and AC-130 vendor/supplier

LORAN—Long-Range Navigation (radio navigation aid)

MM or mm—Millimeter

Moonbeam—Nighttime callsign for ABCCC

Mach—Term used to define the speed of sound (around seven hundred miles an hour at sea level), followed by a multiplier; for example, Mach 3 is roughly three times the speed of sound or twenty-one hundred miles an hour

MRE—Meals Ready to Eat

NOD—Night Observation Device

Orbit—One complete circuit of a pylon turn

PCS—Permanent Change of Station; assigns you to a new base permanently

Pickle—Term used when weapon is launched or released

Pipper—Superimposed aiming dot, circle, or crosshair found in electronic heads-up gunsights.

Pylon Turn—A 360-degree turn flown around a fixed point

R&D—Research and Development

Red X—A symbol used in the aircraft maintenance record indicating that a component is defective to the point that it makes the aircraft not flyable

RTAF—Royal Thai Air Force

SAC—Strategic Air Command

SAM—Surface to Air Missile

Sanitize—The act of removing any patches or other identifying objects from a flight suit to avoid unnecessary or compromising identification

SEA – Southeast Asia

Sparkle—The firing of tracer ammunition for a fighter escort to determine a target's position by visually following tracer to the ground

S&W—Smith and Wesson

STOL—Short takeoff and landing

SUU—Suspended Utility Unit; Any number of externally mounted equipment, usually fitted into pods that are used to carry/shield guns or other auxiliary weapons equipment

TAC—Tactical Air Command

TDY—Temporary Duty; this type of orders assigns you to a new base temporarily

VTOL—Vertical takeoff and landing

Winchester—Term used to indicate when an aircraft has expended all of its ordnance

ACKNOWLEDGEMENTS

———◆———

Atta boys are in order to some very special individuals for their technical and "memory" expertise:

The following folks were part of my crew and have provided photographs, facts, names, and dates of some of our missions. The data provided by these individuals has answered 38 years worth of questions, forgotten memories, and corrected a great deal of misinformation.

Ed Wakeman, my BC operator. Prior to being assigned to the AC-130, Ed was an Electronics Warfare officer and his duties found him flying Top Secret missions on very secret aircraft that very few people knew about. Some of the security we enjoy today is due to the efforts of Ed and his contemporaries during that period. Ed not only helped jog my memory on crew names and other data, he also provided some incredible photos that were very important in describing the damage to the First Lady. Ed is retired and living in the Tampa Bay area.

Larry Michalove, my IR operator. During his stay in Ubon, Larry would write letters home that included bed time stories intended for his children. Years later, his children read the stories to their own children. One of the grandchildren related one of these stories to a teacher. The teacher was so impressed that she suggested Larry publish the stories. He followed through with the suggestion and the award winning book, "The Four Little Children" was published. Larry is retired and living in Alabama.

Ron Bienias, initially my copilot under Col Sam and later my pilot. Ron is currently the President/Owner of Forrest Summit Products in the Chicago area. His recollection of some particular terms and aircraft specific data allowed me to more accurately recreate parts of the story to make them technically correct.

Although never part of my crew, I have to mention Dave Burns, another Spectre gunner, for setting me straight on some of the "urban legend" stories that I'd heard while in Ubon. Dave was a gunner in the original AC-130A program after its inception, and flew in most, if not all, the modified versions through the AC-130H. Dave has also retired and has moved back to Ubon, Thailand.

A special acknowledgement also goes out to the following folks:

Bill Walter, the "God of Guns". Bill was a Spectre gunner during Panama, Grenada, and the Gulf War. Since retiring, Bill has been deeply involved with the R&D of new weapons systems. He is also personally responsible for allowing me to replace Dale Compton's chrome plated 40 mm commemorative shell that was lost or stolen over 20 years ago.

PJ Cook, the Web Master of the Spectre Association. PJ flew as a Spectre gunner during the same time frame as

Bill. PJ was a great source of encouragement for me to begin writing "Hooch Stories" for the Association and put me in contact with the likes of Bill, and others, who would ultimately refresh my memory and give me new technical information on the past and current Gunship programs.

A special thanks to Bill Patterson for consenting to an hour and a half phone interview and setting the record straight about the prop incident on Prometheus. Bill was the IO that night.

And special thanks as well to Tom Combs, the crew chief of Prometheus AND #043, which was shot down in June of 72 with great loss of life. No crew chief should have to endure the loss of two airplanes within 4 months. Tom provided the missing "gap" info for that part of the story.

And finally, the Wikipedia Web Site, for giving me a quick reference source of forgotten words, tech data, and specifics without me having to leave the house.